Jacob's Ladder

Reading Comprehension Program

Second Edition

Grades

6-7

Jacob's Ladder

Second Edition

Grades 6-7

Reading Comprehension Program

Tamra Stambaugh, Ph.D., &
Joyce VanTassel-Baska, Ed.D.

PRUFROCK PRESS INC.
WACO, TEXAS

Prufrock Press Inc.
P.O. Box 8813
Waco, TX 76714-8813
Phone: (800) 998-2208
Fax: (800) 240-0333
http://www.prufrock.com

Part I: Teachers' Guide to Jacob's Ladder Reading Comprehension Program

Introduction to *Jacob's Ladder, Grades 6–7*

Jacob's Ladder, Grades 6–7 (2nd ed.) is a supplemental reading program that implements targeted readings from short stories, poetry, and biographies, building on the work in the previous edition, *Jacob's Ladder, Level 4*. With this program, students engage in an inquiry process that moves from lower order to higher order thinking skills. Starting with basic literary understanding, students learn to critically analyze texts by determining implications and consequences, generalizations, main ideas, and/or creative synthesis. Suggested for students in grades 6–7 to enhance reading comprehension and critical thinking, *Jacob's Ladder, Grades 6–7* tasks are organized into six skill ladders: A–F. Each ladder focuses on a different skill. Students "climb" each ladder by answering lower level to higher level questions or rungs at the top of each ladder. Each ladder stands alone and focuses on a separate critical thinking component in reading. Each genre section (short story, poetry, and biography) includes a culminating activity that allows students the opportunity to compare and contrast different selections in that genre based on specific criteria. Pre- and postassessments are also included for differentiation and to measure student growth, and a culminating activity allows students the opportunity to write and critique their own creative writing work.

Ladder A focuses on implications and consequences. By leading students through sequencing and cause-and-effect activities, they learn to draw implications and consequences from readings. Ladder B focuses on making generalizations. Students first learn to provide details and examples, and then move to classifying and organizing those details in order to make generalizations. Ladder C focuses on main idea, theme, or concept. Students begin by identifying setting and characters and then make inferences about the literary situation. Ladder D focuses on creative synthesis by leading students through paraphrasing and summarizing activities. Ladder E focuses on readers' emotional responses to the literature by understanding emotion, expressing it, and then channeling it productively. Ladder F provides an emphasis on metacognition by engaging learners in reflecting on the literature read and on their own applications of it for their lives. Table 1 provides a visual representation of the six ladders and corresponding objectives for each ladder and rung.

The second editions in the *Jacob's Ladder* series consist of seven levels, divided by grade: K–1, 1–2, 3, 4, 5, 6–7, and 7–8. There are also three nonfiction books focused on grades 3, 4, and 5 (respectively) that include biography study, editorial cartoons and photographs, speeches, and informational text, as well as comparison texts to fiction and nonfiction selections. Most of the fiction-based books contain short stories, poetry, and nonfiction selections, including biographies. Additionally, most of the pieces include at least two commensurate ladders for each selection, with a few exceptions (e.g., the K–1 poetry section and the Grade 3 poetry section, which have one ladder per poem).

Although grade-level distinctions have been set for each of the second editions, teachers may find that they want to vary usage beyond the recommended levels, depending on student abilities. Evidence suggests that the curriculum can be successfully implemented with gifted learners and advanced readers, as well as promising learners, at different grade levels. Thus, the levels vary and overlap to provide opportunities for teachers to select the most appropriate set of readings for meaningful differentiation for their gifted, bright, or promising learners.

Ladder A:
Focus on Implications and Consequences

The goal of Ladder A is to develop prediction and forecasting skills by encouraging students to make connections among the information provided. Starting with sequencing, students learn to recognize basic types of change that occur within a text. Through identifying cause-and-effect relationships, students then can judge the impact of certain events. Finally,

TABLE 1
Goals and Objectives of Jacob's Ladder by Ladder and Rung

Ladder A	Ladder B	Ladder C	Ladder D	Ladder E	Ladder F
A3: Consequences and Implications — Students will be able to predict character actions and story outcomes and make real-world forecasts.	**B3: Generalizations** — Students will be able to make general statements about a reading and/or an idea within the reading, using data to support their statements.	**C3: Main Idea, Theme, or Concept** — Students will be able to identify a major idea or theme common throughout the text.	**D3: Creative Synthesis** — Students will be able to create something new using what they have learned from the reading and their synopses.	**E3: Using Emotion** — Students will be able to analyze how emotion affects the passage and/or the reader.	**F3: Reflecting** — Students will be able to (a) evaluate ideas and plans, (b) provide new plans of action, and (c) explain the pros/cons of a given selection.
A2: Cause and Effect — Students will be able to identify and predict relationships between character behavior and story events and their effects upon other characters or events.	**B2: Classifications** — Students will be able to categorize different aspects of the text or identify and sort categories from a list of topics or details.	**C2: Inference** — Students will be able to use textual clues to read between the lines and make judgments about specific textual events, ideas, or character analysis.	**D2: Summarizing** — Students will be able to provide a synopsis of text sections.	**E2: Expressing Emotion** — Students will be able to articulate their feelings through a variety of media (e.g., song, art, poem, story, essay, speech).	**F2: Monitoring and Assessing** — Students will be able to analyze a plan of action (including implications, consequences, and big ideas) and articulate future goals to accomplish a task.
A1: Sequencing — Students will be able to list, in order of importance or occurrence in the text, specific events or plot summaries.	**B1: Details** — Students will be able to list specific details or recall facts related to the text or generate a list of ideas about a specific topic or character.	**C1: Literary Elements** — Students will be able to identify and explain specific story elements, such as character, setting, or poetic device.	**D1: Paraphrasing** — Students will be able to restate lines read using their own words.	**E1: Understanding Emotion** — Students will be able to explain how emotion and feeling are conveyed in a text and/or their personal experience.	**F1: Planning and Goal Setting** — Students will be able to explain and design an outline or plan given certain stimuli.

through recognizing consequences and implications, students predict future events as logical and identify both short- and long-term consequences by judging probable outcomes based on data provided. The rungs are as follows:

- **Ladder A, Rung 1, Sequencing:** The lowest rung on the ladder, sequencing, requires students to organize a set of information in order, based on their reading (e.g., List the steps of a recipe in order).

- **Ladder A, Rung 2, Cause and Effect:** The middle rung, cause and effect, requires students to think about relationships and identify what causes certain effects and/or what effects were brought about because of certain causes (e.g., What causes a cake to rise in the oven? What effect does the addition of egg yolks have on a batter?).

- **Ladder A, Rung 3, Consequences and Implications:** The highest rung on Ladder A requires students to think about both short- and long-term events that may happen as a result of an effect they have identified (e.g., What are the short- and long-term consequences of baking at home?). Students learn to draw consequences and implications from the text for application in the real world.

Ladder B: Focus on Generalizations

The goal of Ladder B is to help students develop deductive reasoning skills, moving from the concrete elements in a story to abstract ideas. Students begin by learning the importance of concrete details and how they can be organized. By the top rung, students are able to make general statements spanning a topic or concept. The rungs are as follows:

- **Ladder B, Rung 1, Details:** The lowest rung on Ladder B, details, requires students to list examples or details from what they have read and/or to list examples they know from the real world or have read about (e.g., Make a list of types of transportation. Write as many as you can think of in 2 minutes).

- **Ladder B, Rung 2, Classifications:** The middle rung of Ladder B, classifications, focuses on students' ability to categorize examples and details based on characteristics (e.g., How might we categorize the modes of transportation you identified?). This activity builds students' skills in categorization and classification.

- **Ladder B, Rung 3, Generalizations:** The highest rung on Ladder B, generalizations, requires students to use the list and categories generated at Rungs 1 and 2 to develop two to three general statements that apply to *all* of their examples (e.g., Write three statements about transportation).

Ladder C: Focus on Main Ideas, Themes, or Concepts

The goal of Ladder C is to develop literary analysis skills based on an understanding of literary elements. After completing Ladder C, students state the main ideas, themes, or concepts of a text after identifying the setting, characters, and context of the piece. The rungs for this ladder are as follows:

- **Ladder C, Rung 1, Literary Elements:** While working on the lowest rung of Ladder C, literary elements, students identify and/or describe the setting or situation in which the reading occurs. This rung also requires students to develop an understanding of a given character by identifying qualities he or she possesses and comparing these qualities to other characters they have encountered in their reading (e.g., In *Goldilocks and the Three Bears*, what is the situation in which Goldilocks finds herself? What qualities do you admire in Goldilocks? What qualities do you find problematic? How is she similar to or different from other fairy tale characters you have encountered?).

- **Ladder C, Rung 2, Inference:** Inference serves as the middle rung of Ladder C and requires students to think through a situation in the text and come to a conclusion based on the information and clues provided (e.g., What evidence exists that Goldilocks ate the porridge? What inferences can you make about the bears' subsequent action?).

- **Ladder C, Rung 3, Main Idea, Theme, or Concept:** The highest rung of Ladder C, main idea, theme, or concept, requires students to state the central idea or theme for a reading. This exercise necessitates that the students explain an idea from the reading that best states what the text means (e.g., How would you rename the fairy tale? Why? What is the overall theme of *Goldilocks and the Three Bears*? Which morals apply to the fairy tale? Why?).

Ladder D: Focus on Creative Synthesis

The goal of Ladder D is to help students develop skills in creative synthesis in order to foster students' creation of new material based on information from the reading. It moves from the level of restating ideas to creating new ideas about a topic or concept. The rungs are as follows:

- **Ladder D, Rung 1, Paraphrasing:** The lowest rung on Ladder D is paraphrasing. This rung requires students to restate a short passage using their own words (e.g., Rewrite the following quotation in your own words: "But as soon as [the Lion] came near to Androcles, he recognized his friend, and fawned upon him, and licked his hands like a friendly dog. The emperor, surprised at this, summoned Androcles to him, who told the whole story. Whereupon the slave was pardoned and freed, and the Lion let loose to his native forest.").

- **Ladder D, Rung 2, Summarizing:** Summarizing, the middle rung on Ladder D, requires students to summarize larger sections of text by selecting the most important key points within a passage (e.g., Choose one section of the story and summarize it in five sentences).

- **Ladder D, Rung 3, Creative Synthesis:** The highest rung on Ladder D requires students to create something new, using what they have learned from the reading and their synopses of it (e.g., Write another fable about the main idea you identified for this fable, using characters, setting, and a plot of your choice).

Ladder E: Focus on Emotional Development

The goal of Ladder E is to help students develop skills in using their emotional intelligence in order to regulate and modulate behavior with respect to learning. It moves from students' understanding of emotion in themselves and others, to expressing emotion, to channeling emotion for cognitive ends. The rungs are as follows:

- **Ladder E, Rung 1, Understanding Emotion:** The lowest rung on Ladder E is understanding emotion in oneself and others. This requires students to identify emotions in characters and relate them to their own lives (e.g., What feelings does the main character portray throughout the story? How would you compare his temperament to yours?). It also requires them to recognize emotional situations and pinpoint the nature of the emotions involved and what is causing them. Many of the poetry and fiction selections are employed to engage students in the use of this ladder.

- **Ladder E, Rung 2, Expressing Emotion:** The middle rung on Ladder E, expressing emotion, asks students to express emotion in response to their reading of various selections (e.g., The main character seems to worry too much. Is worry ever beneficial? Why or why not?). They may often do this in self-selected formats, including poetry or prose. Teachers may want to substitute kinesthetic responses in the form of dance or skits that demonstrate an emotional reaction to the selections.

- **Ladder E, Rung 3, Using Emotion:** The highest rung on Ladder E, using emotion, encourages students to begin regulating emotion for specific purposes (e.g., How does worry impact your life? What steps can you take to minimize worry? Write a personal action plan). In application to poetry, prose, and biography, students need to demonstrate a clear understanding of how to use emotion effectively for accomplishing specific ends, whether through giving a speech or writing a passionate letter in defense of an idea. The deliberate incorporation of emotion in one's communication is stressed.

Ladder F: Focus on Metacognition

The goal of Ladder F is to help students in planning, monitoring, and evaluating their academic and career goals. Through readings about eminent persons, students examine the impact of various factors that inhibit or enhance personal contributions and trajectories. Then students are asked to apply the new learning to their own individual circumstances and short- and long-term goals. The rungs are as follows:

- **Ladder F, Rung 1, Planning and Goal Setting:** The lowest rung on Ladder F, planning and goal setting, requires students to consider how talented people from all walks of life have deliberately thought about how they will live their lives (e.g., Passion and perseverance are two traits of successful individuals. Describe how this passion and perseverance were evidenced in Bourke-White's life). Through biographical inquiry, students model this behavior in setting their own academic and career goals, based on assessing their interests, aptitudes, and values.

- **Ladder F, Rung 2, Monitoring and Assessing:** The middle rung on Ladder F, monitoring and assessing, requires students to think about their capacity to complete projects and to move forward with goals and outcomes (e.g., What are you passionate about? How can you use that passion for success?). Students are asked to judge the quality of their own products and to assess their own progress toward goals by setting appropriate criteria and then applying them to a situation. By analyzing what eminent individuals have done, students are able to think about the decisions made and the timing of those decisions as they impacted life outcomes.

- **Ladder F, Rung 3, Reflecting:** The highest rung on Ladder F, reflecting, engages students in reflecting on what they have learned from their study of biography and how the principles may apply to their own life planning and career development process (e.g., Write five ways you are successful and five things you need to work on to become more successful. Design a personal growth plan with realistic and achievable goals to become more successful in at least one area of your life). Students are asked to create career plans, to apply the talent development markers to their own lives, and to select the most important aspects of a life for emulation.

Process Skills

Along with the six goals addressed by the ladders, a seventh goal focusing on process skills is incorporated in the *Jacob's Ladder* curriculum. The aim of this goal is to promote learning through interaction and discussion of reading material in the classroom. After completing the ladders and following guidelines for discussion and teacher feedback, students will be able to:

- articulate their understanding of a reading passage using textual support,
- engage in proper dialogue about the meaning of a selection, and
- discuss varied ideas about the intention of a passage both orally and in writing.

Reading Genres and Selections

The reading selections include three major genres: short stories (fables, myths, short stories, and essays), poetry, and biographies. In the Grades

6–7 book, each reading within a genre has been carefully selected or tailored for student reading accessibility and interest. The stories and poems for the *Jacob's Ladder* curriculum at each grade level were chosen with four basic criteria in mind: (1) high-quality writing and richness for interpretation, (2) concrete to abstract development, (3) level of vocabulary, and (4) age-appropriate themes. The readings and exercises are designed to move students forward in their abstract thinking processes by promoting critical and creative thinking. The vocabulary in each reading is grade-level appropriate; however, when new or unfamiliar words are encountered, they should be covered in class before the readings and ladder questions are assigned. Themes also are appropriate to the students' ages at each grade level and were chosen to complement themes typically seen in texts for each particular level. The short stories, poetry, and biography readings with corresponding ladder sets are delineated in Part II. Table 2 outlines all Grades 6–7 readings by genre.

Rationale

Constructing meaning of the written word is one of the earliest tasks required of students in schools. This skill occupies the central place in the curriculum at the elementary level. Yet, approaches to teaching reading comprehension often are "skill and drill," using worksheets on low-level reading material. As a result, students frequently are unable to transfer these skills from exercise pages and apply them to new higher level reading material.

The time expended to ensure that students become autonomous and advanced readers would suggest the need for a methodology that deliberately moves students from simple to complex reading skills with grade-appropriate texts. Such a learning approach to reading skill development ensures that students can traverse easily from basic comprehension skills to higher level critical reading skills, while using the same reading stimulus to navigate this transition. Reading comprehension is enhanced by instructional scaffolding, moving students from lower order to higher order thinking, using strategies and processes to help students analyze passages (Fisher & Frey, 2014; Peterson & Taylor, 2012). In addition, teachers who emphasize higher order thinking through questions and tasks such as those at the higher rungs of each ladder promote greater reading growth (Degener & Berne, 2016). *Jacob's Ladder* was written in response to teacher findings that students needed additional scaffolding to work consistently at higher levels of thinking in reading.

TABLE 2
Jacob's Ladder Grades 6–7 Selections by Genre

Short Stories	Poems	Biographies
The Wolf and the Kid originally told by Aesop	*Weathers* by Thomas Hardy	Erwin Schrödinger, physicist
The Last Lesson by Alphonse Daudet	*Sonnet 73* by William Shakespeare	Amartya Sen, economist
The Mouse by H. H. Munro	*The Clod and the Pebble* by William Blake	Harriet Tubman, social reformer
The Monkey's Paw by W. W. Jacobs	*Hope Is the Thing With Feathers* by Emily Dickinson	Marie Curie, scientist
The Diamond Necklace by Guy de Maupassant	*Joy in the Woods* by Claude McKay	Margaret Mead, anthropologist
The Celebrated Jumping Frog of Calaveras County by Mark Twain	*The Wild Swans at Coole* by William Butler Yeats	Lin-Manuel Miranda, composer, playwright, and lyricist
The Lottery Ticket by Anton Chekhov	*Not They Who Soar* by Paul Laurence Dunbar	

In addition, the adoption of the Common Core State Standards (CCSS) in 2010, or state standards that mimicked the CCSS, resulted in a new emphasis on the close reading of complex text. This involves making annotations, using text-dependent questions, and holding discussions about texts. Harvey and Goudvis (2007) have promoted the use of text coding and annotating as methods for students to deepen comprehension. In order to focus students' attention on specific elements of text in multiple readings, researchers have emphasized the need for teachers to provide text-dependent questions (Fisher & Frey, 2012; Lapp, Grant, Moss, & Johnson, 2013; Santori & Belfatti, 2017). Text-based discussion can facilitate reading comprehension by allowing students to construct their understanding of ideas in collaboration with their classmates (DeFrance & Fahrenbruck, 2015). Researchers have also noted the importance of discussions for enhancing student talk about texts and improving the comprehension of text (Duke, Pearson, Strachan, & Billman, 2011; Lawrence & Snow, 2011). Many of the questions in *Jacob's Ladder* are text-dependent questions, although some ladders and questions promote enrichment as students are also encouraged to go beyond the text to make connections within and across other disciplines. Discussions may be done in dyads, small groups, or with the entire class. Although *Jacob's Ladder* does not specifically address text coding or annotating, those are strategies that could easily be incorporated as students read the selections.

The *Jacob's Ladder* program is a compilation of the instructional scaffolding and reading exercises necessary to aid students in their journey toward becoming critical readers. Students learn concept development skills through learning to generalize, predicting and forecasting skills through delineating implications of events, and literary analysis skills through discerning textual meaning. The questions and tasks for each reading are open-ended, as this type of approach to responding to literature improves performance on comprehension tests (Wasik & Hindman, 2013). Progressing through the hierarchy of skills also requires students to re-read the text, thereby improving metacomprehension accuracy (Hedin & Conderman, 2010).

Research Base

A quasi-experimental study was conducted using *Jacob's Ladder* as a supplementary program for students in Title I schools, grades 3–5. After professional development occurred, experimental teachers were instructed to implement the *Jacob's Ladder* curriculum in addition to their basal reading series and guided reading groups. Teachers in the control group taught their district-adopted textbook reading series as the main curriculum.

Findings from this study ($N = 495$) suggest that when compared to students who used the basal reader only, those students who were exposed to the *Jacob's Ladder* curriculum showed significant gains in reading comprehension and critical thinking. Likewise, students who used the curriculum showed significant and important growth on curriculum-based assessments that included determining implications/consequences, making inferences, outlining themes and generalizations, and applying creative synthesis. Students reported greater interest in reading and noted that the curriculum made them "think harder." Teachers reported more in-depth student discussion and personal growth in the ability to ask open-ended questions when reading (Stambaugh, 2007).

Implementation Considerations

Teachers need to consider certain issues when implementing the *Jacob's Ladder* curriculum. Although the program is targeted for promising students who need more exposure to higher level thinking skills in reading in order to attain higher levels of thinking and access, the program may be suitable for learners who are functioning above or below grade level, depending upon the level of *Jacob's Ladder* used and the amount of support provided by the teacher.

As modeling, coaching, and feedback appear to enhance student growth in reading and writing (Fisher & Frey, 2015), it is recommended that teachers review how to complete the task ladders with the entire class at least once, outlining expectations and record-keeping tasks, as well as modeling the process prior to assigning small-group or independent work. Students should complete the ladder tasks on their own paper or on the template provided in Appendix B. As students gain more confidence in the curriculum, the teacher should allow more independent work coupled with small-group or paired discussion, and then whole-group sharing with teacher feedback. The ladders are not intended to be worksheets that students complete. Instead, each ladder and ladder-rung questions are to be used for discussion and skill-based options that work in tandem to develop students' higher level thinking skills.

Completing these activities in dyads or small groups will facilitate discussions that stress collaborative reasoning, thereby fostering greater engagement and higher level thinking (Duke et al., 2011; Lawrence & Snow, 2011). The stories and accompanying ladder questions and activities also may be organized into a reading center in the classroom or utilized with reading groups during guided reading as part of a differentiated reading program.

The Learning Process of Jacob's Ladder

The process of inquiry and feedback, as led and modeled by the teacher, is critical to the success of the program and student mastery of process skills. Teachers need to solicit multiple student responses and encourage dialogue about various perspectives and interpretations of a given text, requiring students to justify their answers with textual support and concrete examples (VanTassel-Baska & Stambaugh, 2006a, 2006b). Sample follow-up questions and prompts such as those listed below can be used by the teacher and posted in the classroom to guide student discussion.

- That's interesting; does anyone have a different idea?
- What in the story makes you say that?
- What do you think the author means by . . . ?
- What do you think are the implications or consequences of . . . ?
- Did anyone view that differently? How?
- Does anyone have a different point of view? Justify your answer.

- In the story I noticed that . . . Do you think that might have significance to the overall meaning?

- I heard someone say that they thought the poem (story) was about . . . What do you think? Justify your answer from the events of the story.

- Do you notice any key words that might be significant? Why?

- Do you notice any words that give you a mental picture? Do those words have significance? What might they symbolize?

- I agree with . . . because . . .

- I had a different idea than . . . because . . .

Grouping Students

Jacob's Ladder may be used in a number of different grouping patterns. The program should be introduced initially as a whole-group activity directed by the teacher with appropriate open-ended questions, feedback, and monitoring. After students have examined each type of ladder with teacher guidance, they should be encouraged to use the program by writing ideas independently, sharing with a partner, and then discussing the findings with a group. The dyad approach provides maximum opportunities for student discussion of the readings and collaborative decisions about the answers to questions posed. One purpose of the program is to solicit meaningful discussion of the text, which is best accomplished in small groups of students at similar reading levels (VanTassel-Baska & Little, 2017). Research continues to support instructional grouping in reading as an important part of successful implementation of a program (Rogers, 2002).

Demonstrating Growth: Pre- and Postassessments and Student Products

The pre- and postassessments included in Appendix A were designed as a diagnostic-prescriptive approach to guide program implementation of *Jacob's Ladder*. The pretest should be administered, scored, and then used to guide student instruction and the selection of readings for varied ability groups. Both the pre- and postassessment and scoring rubric for each rubric category and level are included in Appendix A.

In both the pre- and postassessments, students read a short passage and respond to the four questions. Question 1 focuses on consequences and implications (Ladder A), Question 2 on inference (Ladder C), Question 3 on generalization, theme, and concept (Ladders B and C), and Question 4 on creative synthesis (Ladder D). By analyzing each question and scored response, teachers may select the appropriate readings and ladders based on student need.

Upon conclusion of the program or as a midpoint check, the posttest may be administered to compare the pretest results and to measure growth in students' responses. These pre-post results could be used as part of a student portfolio, in a parent-teacher conference, or as documentation of curriculum effectiveness and student progress. The pre- and postassessments were piloted to ensure pre-post equivalent forms reliability (a = .76) and interrater reliability (a = .81).

Student Reflection, Feedback, and Record Keeping

Students may use an answer sheet, such as the one provided in Appendix B, for each ladder to record their personal thoughts independently before discussing them with a partner. After finishing the ladders for each reading selection, a reflection page (also in Appendix B) can be provided, asking for each student's personal assessment of the work completed. Teachers also will want to check student answers as ladder segments are completed and conduct an individual or small-group consultation to ensure that students understand why their answers may be effective or ineffective. In order to analyze student responses and progress across the program, teachers need to monitor student performance, using the student answer sheets to indicate appropriate completion of tasks. Specific comments about student work also are important to promote growth and understanding of content.

Record-keeping sheets for the class are also provided in Appendix B. On these forms, teachers record student progress on a 3-point scale: 2 (*applies skills very effectively*), 1 (*understands and applies skills*), or 0 (*needs more practice with the given skill set*) across readings and ladder sets. This form can be used as part of a diagnostic-prescriptive approach to selecting reading materials and ladders based on student understanding or the need for more practice.

Sample Concluding Activities: Ideas for Grading

Grading the ladders and responses is at the teacher's discretion. Teachers should not overemphasize the lower rungs in graded activities. Lower rungs are intended only as a vehicle to the higher level questions at the top of the ladder. Instead, top-rung questions may be used as a journal prompt or as part of a graded, open-ended writing response. Grades also could be given based on guided discussion after students are trained on appropriate ways to discuss literature. Additional ideas for grading are as follows:

- Write a persuasive essay to justify your understanding of the story.

- Create a symbol to show the meaning of the story. Write two sentences to justify your symbol.

- In one word or phrase, what is this story mostly about? Justify your answer using examples from the story.

- Write a letter from the author's point of view, explaining what the meaning of the story is to young children and keeping with the same theme.

- Pretend you are an illustrator and need to create a drawing for the story or poem that shows what the story or poem is mostly about. Write a sentence to describe your illustration and why it is the best option.

- You have been reading biographies of eminent people in many fields. Select one and discuss how one's life choices, internal characteristics, and circumstances impact his or her career trajectory.

- The importance of emotion in storytelling cannot be overstressed. Analyze a favorite story according to its emotional content and how it contributed to your liking the story, include literary features of the text that support how the author created tone and mood.

- Compare and contrast two stories, poems, or biographies, including how the author uses different literary elements to contribute to the theme.

- Select two different stories or poems with a similar theme and explain how that theme is developed.

Culminating activities are also included at the end of each genre section so that students can reflect upon the previous readings and compare and contrast them in a variety of ways based on their new learning. These culminating activities could also be graded.

Time Allotment

Although the time needed to complete *Jacob's Ladder* tasks will vary by student, most lessons should take students 15–30 minutes to read the selection and another 15–20 minutes to complete one ladder individually. More time is required for paired student and whole-group discussion of the questions. Teachers may wish to set aside 2 days each week for focusing on one *Jacob's Ladder* reading and its commensurate ladders, especially when introducing the program.

Answer Sets

Because the questions are highly individualized and open-ended, no answer sets are given. Students should be encouraged to seek out the levels of meaning in rich text, looking for multiple answers that reflect their own experience and accurate interpretation. Teachers may choose to seek additional sources online for textual interpretations, as needed.

Alignment to Standards

Appendix C contains alignment charts to demonstrate the connection of the fiction and nonfiction reading materials to relevant national standards. One of the benefits of this program is its ability to provide cross-disciplinary coverage of standards through the use of a single reading stimulus. Connections to science and social studies standards are noted. Alignment to the Common Core State Standards in English Language Arts has been used as the basis for the analysis.

References

DeFrance, N. L., & Fahrenbruck, M. L. (2015). Constructing a plan for text-based discussion. *Journal of Adolescent & Adult Literacy, 59*, 575–585. doi:10.1002/jaal.477

Degener, S., & Berne, J. (2016). Complex questions promote complex thinking. *The Reading Teacher, 70*, 595–599. doi:10.1002/trtr.1535

Duke, N. K., Pearson, P. D., Strachan, S. L., & Billman, A. K. (2011). Essential elements of fostering and teaching reading comprehension. In S. J. Samuels & A. E. Farstrup (Eds.), *What research has to say about reading instruction* (pp. 51–93). Newark, DE: International Reading Association. doi:10.1598/0829.03

Fisher, D., & Frey, N. (2012). Close reading in elementary schools. *The Reading Teacher, 66*, 179–188. doi:10.1002/TRTR.01117

Fisher, D., & Frey, N. (2014). Scaffolded reading instruction of content-area texts. *The Reading Teacher, 67*, 347–351. doi:10.1002/trtr.1234

Fisher, D., & Frey, N. (2015). Teacher modeling using complex informational texts. *The Reading Teacher, 69*(1), 63–69. doi:10.1002/trtr.1372

Harvey, S., & Goudvis, A. (2007). *Strategies that work: Teaching comprehension for understanding and engagement* (2nd ed.). Portland, ME: Stenhouse Publishers.

Hedin, L. R., & Conderman, G. (2010). Teaching students to comprehend informational text through rereading. *The Reading Teacher, 63*, 556–565. doi:10.1598/RT.63.7.3

Lapp, D., Grant, M., Moss, B., & Johnson, K. (2013). Close reading of science texts: What's now? What's next? *The Reading Teacher, 67*, 109–119.

Lawrence, J. F., & Snow, C. E. (2011). Oral discourse and reading. In M. L. Kamil, P. D. Pearson, E. B. Moje, & P. P. Afflerbach (Eds.), *Handbook of reading research* (Vol. 4, pp. 320–337). New York, NY: Routledge.

Peterson, D. S., & Taylor, B. M. (2012). Using higher order questioning to accelerate students' growth in reading. *The Reading Teacher, 65*, 295–304. doi:10.1002/TRTR.01045

Rogers, K. (2002). *Re-forming gifted education: How parents and teachers can match the program to the child.* Scottsdale, AZ: Great Potential Press.

Santori, D., & Belfatti, M. (2017). Do text-dependent questions need to be teacher-dependent? Close reading from another angle. *The Reading Teacher, 70*, 649–657. doi:10.1002/trtr.1555

Stambaugh, T. (2007). *Effects of the Jacob's Ladder Reading Comprehension Program* (Unpublished doctoral dissertation). William & Mary, Williamsburg, VA.

VanTassel-Baska, J., & Little, C. (Eds.). (2017). *Content-based curriculum for high-ability learners* (3rd ed.). Waco, TX: Prufrock Press.

VanTassel-Baska, J., & Stambaugh, T. (2006a). *Comprehensive curriculum for gifted learners* (3rd ed.). Needham Heights, MA: Allyn & Bacon.

VanTassel-Baska, J., & Stambaugh, T. (2006b). Project Athena: A pathway to advanced literacy development for children of poverty. *Gifted Child Today, 29*(2), 58–65.

Wasik, B. A., & Hindman, A. H. (2013). Realizing the promise of open-ended questions. *The Reading Teacher, 67,* 302–311. doi:10.1002/trtr.1218

Part II: Readings and Student Ladder Sets

Chapter 1: Short Stories and Corresponding Ladders
Chapter 2: Poetry and Corresponding Ladders
Chapter 3: Biographies and Corresponding Ladders

Short Stories

Chapter 1 includes the selected readings and accompanying question sets for each short story selection. Each reading is followed by two or three sets of questions; each set is aligned to one of the six sets of ladder skills.

For *Jacob's Ladder, Grades 6–7*, the skills covered by each selection are as follows:

Title	Ladder Skills
The Wolf and the Kid	D, E
The Last Lesson	A, C, E
The Mouse	A, C, E
The Monkey's Paw	A, B, D
The Diamond Necklace	A, C, E
The Celebrated Jumping Frog of Calaveras County	A, C, D
The Lottery Ticket	B, C, E

The Wolf and the Kid

Originally told by Aesop

A Kid was perched up on the top of a house, and looking down saw a Wolf passing under him. Immediately he began to revile and attack his enemy. "Murderer and thief," he cried, "what are you doing here near honest folks' houses? How dare you make an appearance where your vile deeds are known?"

"Curse away, my young friend," said the Wolf. "It is easy to be brave from a safe distance."

Creative Synthesis

D3

Write a present-day fable that has the same life lesson.

Summarizing

D2

What symbol or word best summarizes the message of the fable? How do you know?

Paraphrasing

D1

In your own words, explain what is meant by "It is easy to be brave from a safe distance."

THE WOLF AND THE KID

THE WOLF AND THE KID

Using Emotion

E3

What advice would you give someone who felt
like he or she was in a no-win situation?

Expressing Emotion

E2

What steps can you take to become less wolf-like or kid-like? List them.

Understanding Emotion

E1

Are you more like the wolf or the kid in real life?

The Last Lesson

By Alphonse Daudet

I started for school very late that morning and was in great dread of a scolding, especially because M. Hamel had said that he would question us on participles, and I did not know the first word about them. For a moment I thought of running away and spending the day out of doors. It was so warm, so bright! The birds were chirping at the edge of the woods; and in the open field back of the sawmill the Prussian soldiers were drilling. It was all much more tempting than the rule for participles, but I had the strength to resist, and hurried off to school.

When I passed the town hall there was a crowd in front of the bulletin-board. For the last two years all our bad news had come from there—the lost battles, the draft, the orders of the commanding officer—and I thought to myself, without stopping:

"What can be the matter now?"

Then, as I hurried by as fast as I could go, the blacksmith, Wachter, who was there, with his apprentice, reading the bulletin, called after me:

"Don't go so fast, bub; you'll get to your school in plenty of time!"

I thought he was making fun of me, and reached M. Hamel's little garden all out of breath.

Usually, when school began, there was a great bustle, which could be heard out in the street, the opening and closing of desks, lessons repeated in unison, very loud, with our hands over our ears to understand better, and the teacher's great ruler rapping on the table. But now it was all so still! I had counted on the commotion to get to my desk without being seen; but, of course, that day everything had to be as quiet as Sunday morning. Through the window I saw my classmates, already in their places, and M. Hamel walking up and down with his terrible iron ruler under his arm. I had to open the door and go in before everybody. You can imagine how I blushed and how frightened I was.

But nothing happened. M. Hamel saw me and said very kindly:

"Go to your place quickly, little Franz. We were beginning without you."

I jumped over the bench and sat down at my desk. Not till then, when I had got a little over my fright, did I see that our teacher had on his beautiful green coat, his frilled shirt, and the little black silk cap, all embroidered, that he never wore except on inspection and prize days. Besides, the whole school seemed so strange and solemn. But the thing that surprised me most was to see, on the back benches that were always empty, the village people sitting quietly like ourselves; old Hauser, with his three-cornered hat, the former mayor, the former postmaster, and several others besides. Everybody looked sad; and Hauser had brought an old primer, thumbed at the edges, and he held it open on his knees with his great spectacles lying across the pages.

While I was wondering about it all, M. Hamel mounted his chair, and, in the same grave and gentle tone which he had used to me, said:

"My children, this is the last lesson I shall give you. The order has come from Berlin to teach only German in the schools of Alsace and Lorraine. The new master comes to-morrow. This is your last French lesson. I want you to be very attentive."

What a thunderclap these words were to me!

Oh, the wretches; that was what they had put up at the town-hall!

My last French lesson! Why, I hardly knew how to write! I should never learn any more! I must stop there, then! Oh, how sorry I was for not learning my lessons, for seeking birds' eggs, or going sliding on the Saar! My books, that had seemed such a nuisance a while ago, so heavy to carry, my grammar, and my history of the saints, were old friends now that I couldn't give up. And M. Hamel, too; the idea that he was going away, that I should never see him again, made me forget all about his ruler and how cranky he was.

Poor man! It was in honor of this last lesson that he had put on his fine Sunday clothes, and now I understood why the old men of the village were sitting there in the back of the room. It was because they were sorry, too, that they had not gone to school more. It was their way of thanking our master for his forty years of faithful service and of showing their respect for the country that was theirs no more.

While I was thinking of all this, I heard my name called. It was my turn to recite. What would I not have given to be able to say that dreadful rule for the participle all through, very loud and clear, and without one mistake? But I got mixed up on the first words and stood there, holding on to my desk, my heart beating, and not daring to look up. I heard M. Hamel say to me:

"I won't scold you, little Franz; you must feel bad enough. See how it is! Every day we have said to ourselves: 'Bah! I've plenty of time. I'll learn it to-morrow.' And now you see where we've come out. Ah, that's the great trouble with Alsace; she puts off learning till to-morrow. Now those fellows out there will have the right to say to you: 'How is it; you pretend to be Frenchmen, and yet you can neither speak nor write your own language?' But you are not the worst, poor little Franz. We've all a great deal to reproach ourselves with.

"Your parents were not anxious enough to have you learn. They pre-ferred to put you to work on a farm or at the mills, so as to have a little more money. And I? I've been to blame also. Have I not often sent you to water my flowers instead of learning your lessons? And when I wanted to go fishing, did I not just give you a holiday?"

Then, from one thing to another, M. Hamel went on to talk of the French language, saying that it was the most beautiful language in the world—the clearest, the most logical; that we must guard it among us and never forget it, because when a people are enslaved, as long as they hold fast to their language it is as if they had the key to their prison. Then he opened a grammar and read us our lesson. I was amazed to see how well I understood it. All he said seemed so easy, so easy! I think, too, that I had never listened so carefully, and that he had never explained everything with so much patience. It seemed almost as if the poor man wanted to give us all he knew before going away, and to put it all into our heads at one stroke.

After the grammar, we had a lesson in writing. That day M. Hamel had new copies for us, written in a beautiful round hand: France, Alsace, France, Alsace. They looked like little flags floating everywhere in the school-room, hung from the rod at the top of our desks. You ought to have seen how every one set to work, and how quiet it was! The only sound was the scratching of the pens over the paper. Once some beetles flew in; but nobody paid any attention to them, not even the littlest ones, who worked right on tracing their fish-hooks, as if that was French, too. On the roof the pigeons cooed very low, and I thought to myself:

"Will they make them sing in German, even the pigeons?"

Whenever I looked up from my writing I saw M. Hamel sitting motion-less in his chair and gazing first at one thing, then at another, as if he wanted to fix in his mind just how everything looked in that little school-room. Fancy! For forty years he had been there in the same place, with his garden outside the window and his class in front of him, just like that. Only the desks and benches had been worn smooth; the walnut-trees in the gar-den were taller, and the hopvine that he had planted himself twined about the windows to the roof. How it must have broken his heart to leave it all, poor man; to hear his sister moving about in the room above, packing their trunks! For they must leave the country next day.

But he had the courage to hear every lesson to the very last. After the writing, we had a lesson in history, and then the babies chanted their ba, be, bi, bo, bu. Down there at the back of the room old Hauser had put on his spectacles and, holding his primer in both hands, spelled the letters with them. You could see that he, too, was crying; his voice trembled with emotion, and it was so funny to hear him that we all wanted to laugh and cry. Ah, how well I remember it, that last lesson!

All at once the church-clock struck 12. Then the Angelus. At the same moment the trumpets of the Prussians, returning from drill, sounded under our windows. M. Hamel stood up, very pale, in his chair. I never saw him look so tall.

"My friends," said he, "I—I—" But something choked him. He could not go on.

Then he turned to the blackboard, took a piece of chalk, and, bearing on with all his might, he wrote as large as he could:

"Vive La France!"

Then he stopped and leaned his head against the wall, and, without a word, he made a gesture to us with his hand:

"School is dismissed—you may go."

A3

Consequences and Implications

What are the implications of culture on literary works in general? Defend your answer using examples from this story and others you have read.

A2

Cause and Effect

What effects did the culture of the day have on the author? How did he portray this in his writing?

A1

Sequencing

Find out more about the French and Prussian war. Sequence the events of the war and its impact on each side.

Main Idea, Theme, or Concept

C3

What is the central theme Daudet is trying
to convey? Defend your answer.

Inference

C2

What is the significance of the French lesson on the
meaning of the story? Why didn't the author use
another subject such as history or math?

Literary Elements

C1

Why do you think Daudet chose to convey his story
through the point of view of a young boy?

THE LAST LESSON

Using Emotion

E3

Does the writer shape the culture or does the culture shape the writer? Defend your answer using evidence from the story as well as other stories you have read from specific time periods.

Expressing Emotion

E2

Consider a major event that has occurred in the U.S. during your lifetime. Write a short story from the point of view of an ordinary person to make sense of the event. Create a Venn diagram to compare your story to Daudet's.

Understanding Emotion

E1

Which literary elements are most prevalent in conveying emotion in the story? Use specific phrases and literary examples to explain your ideas.

THE LAST LESSON

The Mouse

By H. H. Munro

Theodoric Voler had been brought up, from infancy to the confines of middle age, by a fond mother whose chief solicitude had been to keep him screened from what she called the coarser realities of life. When she died she left Theodoric alone in a world that was as real as ever, and a good deal coarser than he considered it had any need to be. To a man of his temperament and upbringing even a simple railway journey was crammed with petty annoyances and minor discords, and as he settled himself down in a second class compartment one September morning he was conscious of ruffled feelings and general mental discomposure. He had been staying at a country vicarage, the inmates of which had been certainly neither brutal nor bacchanalian, but their supervision of the domestic establishment had been of that lax order which invites disaster. The pony carriage that was to take him to the station had never been properly ordered, and when the moment for his departure drew near the handy-man who should have produced the required article was nowhere to be found. In this emergency Theodoric, to his mute but very intense disgust, found himself obliged to collaborate with the vicar's daughter in the task of harnessing the pony, which necessitated groping about in an ill-lighted outhouse called a stable, and smelling very like one—except in patches where it smelt of mice. Without being actually afraid of mice, Theodoric classed them among the coarser incidents of life, and considered that Providence, with a little exercise of moral courage, might long ago have recognised that they were not indispensable, and have withdrawn them from circulation. As the train glided out of the station Theodoric's nervous imagination accused himself of exhaling a weak odour of stable-yard, and possibly of displaying a mouldy straw or two on his usually well-brushed garments. Fortunately the only other occupant of the compartment, a lady of about the same age as himself, seemed inclined for slumber rather than scrutiny; the train was not due to stop till the terminus was reached, in about an hour's time, and the carriage was of the old-fashioned sort, that held no communication with a corridor, therefore no further travelling companions were likely to intrude on Theodoric's semi-privacy. And yet the train had scarcely attained its normal speed before he became reluctantly but vividly aware that he was not alone with the slumbering lady; he was not even alone in his own clothes. A warm, creeping movement over his flesh betrayed the unwelcome and highly resented presence, unseen but poignant, of a strayed mouse, that had evidently dashed into its present retreat during the episode of the pony harnessing. Furtive stamps and shakes and wildly directed pinches failed to dislodge the intruder, whose motto, indeed, seemed to be Excelsior; and the lawful occupant of the clothes lay back against the cushions and endeavoured rapidly to evolve some means for putting an end to the dual ownership. It was unthinkable that he should continue for the space of a whole hour in the horrible position of a Rowton House for vagrant mice (already his imagination had at least doubled the numbers of the alien invasion). On the other hand, nothing less drastic than partial disrobing would ease him of his tormentor, and to undress in the presence of a lady, even for so laudable a purpose, was an idea that made his eartips tingle in a blush of abject shame. He had never been able to bring himself even to the mild exposure of open-work socks in the presence of the fair sex. And yet—the lady in this case was to all appearances soundly and securely asleep; the mouse, on the other hand, seemed to be trying to crowd a Wanderjahr into a few strenuous minutes. If there is any truth in the theory of transmigration, this particular mouse must certainly have been in a former state a member of the Alpine Club. Sometimes in its eagerness it lost its footing and slipped for half an inch or so; and then, in fright, or more probably temper, it bit. Theodoric was goaded into the most audacious undertaking of his life. Crimsoning to the hue of a beetroot and keeping an agonised watch on his slumbering fellow-traveller, he swiftly and noiselessly secured the ends of his railway-rug to the racks on either side of the carriage, so that a substantial curtain hung athwart the compartment. In the narrow dressing-room that he had thus improvised he proceeded with violent haste to extricate himself partially and the mouse entirely from the surrounding casings of tweed and half-wool. As the unravelled mouse gave a wild leap to the floor, the rug, slipping its fastening at either end, also came down with a heart-curdling flop, and almost simultaneously the awakened sleeper opened her eyes. With a movement almost quicker than the mouse's, Theodoric pounced on the rug, and hauled its ample folds chin-high over his dismantled person as he collapsed into the further corner of the carriage. The blood raced and beat in the veins of his neck and forehead, while he waited dumbly for the communication-cord to be pulled. The lady, however, contented herself with a silent stare at her strangely muffled companion. How much had she seen, Theodoric queried to himself, and in any case what on earth must she think of his present posture?

"I think I have caught a chill," he ventured desperately.

"Really, I'm sorry," she replied. "I was just going to ask you if you would open this window."

"I fancy it's malaria," he added, his teeth chattering slightly, as much from fright as from a desire to support his theory.

"I've got some brandy in my hold-all, if you'll kindly reach it down for me," said his companion.

"Not for worlds—I mean, I never take anything for it," he assured her earnestly.

"I suppose you caught it in the Tropics?"

Theodoric, whose acquaintance with the Tropics was limited to an annual present of a chest of tea from an uncle in Ceylon, felt that even the malaria was slipping from him. Would it be possible, he wondered, to disclose the real state of affairs to her in small installments?

"Are you afraid of mice?" he ventured, growing, if possible, more scarlet in the face.

"Not unless they came in quantities, like those that ate up Bishop Hatto. Why do you ask?"

"I had one crawling inside my clothes just now," said Theodoric in a voice that hardly seemed his own. "It was a most awkward situation."

"It must have been, if you wear your clothes at all tight," she observed; "but mice have strange ideas of comfort."

"I had to get rid of it while you were asleep," he continued; then, with a gulp, he added, "it was getting rid of it that brought me to—to this."

"Surely leaving off one small mouse wouldn't bring on a chill," she exclaimed, with a levity that Theodoric accounted abominable.

Evidently she had detected something of his predicament, and was enjoying his confusion. All the blood in his body seemed to have mobilised in one concentrated blush, and an agony of abasement, worse than a myriad mice, crept up and down over his soul. And then, as reflection began to assert itself, sheer terror took the place of humiliation. With every minute that passed the train was rushing nearer to the crowded and bustling terminus where dozens of prying eyes would be exchanged for the one paralysing pair that watched him from the further corner of the carriage. There was one slender despairing chance, which the next few minutes must decide. His fellow-traveller might relapse into a blessed slumber. But as the minutes throbbed by that chance ebbed away. The furtive glance which Theodoric stole at her from time to time disclosed only an unwinking wakefulness.

"I think we must be getting near now," she presently observed.

Name: _____ Date: _____

Theodoric had already noted with growing terror the recurring stacks of small, ugly dwellings that heralded the journey's end. The words acted as a signal. Like a hunted beast breaking cover and dashing madly towards some other haven of momentary safety he threw aside his rug, and struggled frantically into his dishevelled garments. He was conscious of dull suburban stations racing past the window, of a choking, hammering sensation in his throat and heart, and of an icy silence in that corner towards which he dared not look. Then as he sank back in his seat, clothed and almost delirious, the train slowed down to a final crawl, and the woman spoke.

"Would you be so kind," she asked, "as to get me a porter to put me into a cab? It's a shame to trouble you when you're feeling unwell, but being blind makes one so helpless at a railway station."

A3

Consequences and Implications

What message does the author want to convey
to his readers based on this story?

A2

Cause and Effect

How did the sequence of events help us understand the meaning of
the story? For example, why did the author begin with the story of the
boy's background, then put the man on a train, and end with revealing
the lady was blind? How are these events important to the meaning?

A1

Sequencing

Sequence the top six events in the story. Justify
why those events are most important.

THE MOUSE

Main Idea, Theme, or Concept

C3

Who do you think was more blind, the man or the woman?
Explain your answer, using evidence from the story.

Inference

C2

Why do you think the author included a blind woman as a secondary
character? How does that impact the meaning of this story?

Literary Elements

C1

Explain how symbolism was used in the story. Cite specific examples.

THE MOUSE

Using Emotion

E3

What advice would you give the man, based on his previous experiences and actions? Write a short letter of advice to him, using examples from the story as evidence for your suggested changes.

Expressing Emotion

E2

Do you think the man was more self-centered or self-conscious? What evidence in the story supports your answer?

Understanding Emotion

E1

What feelings does the main character portray throughout the story? How would you compare his temperament to yours? Cite specific examples.

THE MOUSE

The Monkey's Paw

By W. W. Jacobs

I

Without, the night was cold and wet, but in the small parlour of Laburnam Villa the blinds were drawn and the fire burned brightly. Father and son were at chess, the former, who possessed ideas about the game involving radical changes, putting his king into such sharp and unnecessary perils that it even provoked comment from the white-haired old lady knitting placidly by the fire.

"Hark at the wind," said Mr. White, who, having seen a fatal mistake after it was too late, was amiably desirous of preventing his son from seeing it.

"I'm listening," said the latter, grimly surveying the board as he stretched out his hand. "Check."

"I should hardly think that he'd come to-night," said his father, with his hand poised over the board.

"Mate," replied the son.

"That's the worst of living so far out," bawled Mr. White, with sudden and unlooked-for violence; "of all the beastly, slushy, out-of-the-way places to live in, this is the worst. Pathway's a bog, and the road's a torrent. I don't know what people are thinking about. I suppose because only two houses on the road are let, they think it doesn't matter."

"Never mind, dear," said his wife soothingly; "perhaps you'll win the next one."

Mr. White looked up sharply, just in time to intercept a knowing glance between mother and son. The words died away on his lips, and he hid a guilty grin in his thin grey beard.

"There he is," said Herbert White, as the gate banged to loudly and heavy footsteps came toward the door.

The old man rose with hospitable haste, and opening the door, was heard condoling with the new arrival. The new arrival also condoled with himself, so that Mrs. White said, "Tut, tut!" and coughed gently as her husband entered the room, followed by a tall burly man, beady of eye and rubicund of visage.

"Sergeant-Major Morris," he said, introducing him.

The sergeant-major shook hands, and taking the proffered seat by the fire, watched contentedly while his host got out whisky and tumblers and stood a small copper kettle on the fire.

At the third glass his eyes got brighter, and he began to talk, the little family circle regarding with eager interest this visitor from distant parts, as he squared his broad shoulders in the chair and spoke of strange scenes and doughty deeds; of wars and plagues and strange peoples.

"Twenty-one years of it," said Mr. White, nodding at his wife and son. "When he went away he was a slip of a youth in the warehouse. Now look at him."

"He don't look to have taken much harm," said Mrs. White, politely.

"I'd like to go to India myself," said the old man, "just to look round a bit, you know."

"Better where you are," said the sergeant-major, shaking his head. He put down the empty glass, and sighing softly, shook it again.

"I should like to see those old temples and fakirs and jugglers," said the old man. "What was that you started telling me the other day about a monkey's paw or something, Morris?"

"Nothing," said the soldier hastily. "Leastways, nothing worth hearing."

"Monkey's paw?" said Mrs. White curiously.

"Well, it's just a bit of what you might call magic, perhaps," said the sergeant-major off-handedly.

His three listeners leaned forward eagerly. The visitor absentmindedly put his empty glass to his lips and then set it down again. His host filled it for him.

"To look at," said the sergeant-major, fumbling in his pocket, "it's just an ordinary little paw, dried to a mummy."

He took something out of his pocket and proffered it. Mrs. White drew back with a grimace, but her son, taking it, examined it curiously.

"And what is there special about it?" inquired Mr. White, as he took it from his son and, having examined it, placed it upon the table.

"It had a spell put on it by an old fakir," said the sergeant-major, "a very holy man. He wanted to show that fate ruled people's lives, and that those who interfered with it did so to their sorrow. He put a spell on it so that three separate men could each have three wishes from it."

His manner was so impressive that his hearers were conscious that their light laughter jarred somewhat.

"Well, why don't you have three, sir?" said Herbert White cleverly.

The soldier regarded him in the way that middle age is wont to regard presumptuous youth. "I have," he said quietly, and his blotchy face whitened.

"And did you really have the three wishes granted?" asked Mrs. White.

"I did," said the sergeant-major, and his glass tapped against his strong teeth.

"And has anybody else wished?" inquired the old lady.

"The first man had his three wishes, yes," was the reply. "I don't know what the first two were, but the third was for death. That's how I got the paw."

His tones were so grave that a hush fell upon the group.

"If you've had your three wishes, it's no good to you now, then, Morris," said the old man at last. "What do you keep it for?"

The soldier shook his head. "Fancy, I suppose," he said slowly.

"If you could have another three wishes," said the old man, eyeing him keenly, "would you have them?"

"I don't know," said the other. "I don't know."

He took the paw, and dangling it between his front finger and thumb, suddenly threw it upon the fire. White, with a slight cry, stooped down and snatched it off.

"Better let it burn," said the soldier solemnly.

"If you don't want it, Morris," said the old man, "give it to me."

"I won't," said his friend doggedly. "I threw it on the fire. If you keep it, don't blame me for what happens. Pitch it on the fire again, like a sensible man."

The other shook his head and examined his new possession closely. "How do you do it?" he inquired.

"Hold it up in your right hand and wish aloud," said the sergeant-major, "but I warn you of the consequences."

"Sounds like the Arabian Nights," said Mrs. White, as she rose and began to set the supper. "Don't you think you might wish for four pairs of hands for me?"

Her husband drew the talisman from his pocket and then all three burst into laughter as the sergeant-major, with a look of alarm on his face, caught him by the arm.

"If you must wish," he said gruffly, "wish for something sensible."

Mr. White dropped it back into his pocket, and placing chairs, motioned his friend to the table. In the business of supper the talisman was partly forgotten, and afterward the three sat listening in an enthralled fashion to a second installment of the soldier's adventures in India.

"If the tale about the monkey paw is not more truthful than those he has been telling us," said Herbert, as the door closed behind their guest, just in time for him to catch the last train, "we shan't make much out of it."

"Did you give him anything for it, father?" inquired Mrs. White, regarding her husband closely.

"A trifle," said he, colouring slightly. "He didn't want it, but I made him take it. And he pressed me again to throw it away."

"Likely," said Herbert, with pretended horror. "Why, we're going to be rich, and famous, and happy. Wish to be an emperor, father, to begin with; then you can't be henpecked."

He darted round the table, pursued by the maligned Mrs. White armed with an antimacassar.

Mr. White took the paw from his pocket and eyed it dubiously. "I don't know what to wish for, and that's a fact," he said slowly. "It seems to me I've got all I want."

"If you only cleared the house, you'd be quite happy, wouldn't you?" said Herbert, with his hand on his shoulder. "Well, wish for two hundred pounds, then; that'll just do it."

His father, smiling shamefacedly at his own credulity, held up the talisman, as his son, with a solemn face somewhat marred by a wink at his mother, sat down at the piano and struck a few impressive chords.

"I wish for two hundred pounds," said the old man distinctly.

A fine crash from the piano greeted the words, interrupted by a shuddering cry from the old man. His wife and son ran toward him.

"It moved," he cried, with a glance of disgust at the object as it lay on the floor. "As I wished it twisted in my hands like a snake."

"Well, I don't see the money," said his son, as he picked it up and placed it on the table, "and I bet I never shall."

"It must have been your fancy, father," said his wife, regarding him anxiously.

He shook his head. "Never mind, though; there's no harm done, but it gave me a shock all the same."

They sat down by the fire again while the two men finished their pipes. Outside, the wind was higher than ever, and the old man started nervously at the sound of a door banging upstairs. A silence unusual and depressing settled upon all three, which lasted until the old couple rose to retire for the night.

"I expect you'll find the cash tied up in a big bag in the middle of your bed," said Herbert, as he bade them good-night, "and something horrible squatting up on top of the wardrobe watching you as you pocket your ill-gotten gains."

He sat alone in the darkness, gazing at the dying fire, and seeing faces in it. The last face was so horrible and so simian that he gazed at it in amazement. It got so vivid that, with a little uneasy laugh, he felt on the table for a glass containing a little water to throw over it. His hand grasped the monkey's paw, and with a little shiver he wiped his hand on his coat and went up to bed.

II

In the brightness of the wintry sun next morning as it streamed over the breakfast table Herbert laughed at his fears. There was an air of prosaic wholesomeness about the room which it had lacked on the previous night, and the dirty, shrivelled little paw was pitched on the sideboard with a carelessness which betokened no great belief in its virtues.

"I suppose all old soldiers are the same," said Mrs. White. "The idea of our listening to such nonsense! How could wishes be granted in these days? And if they could, how could two hundred pounds hurt you, father?"

"Might drop on his head from the sky," said the frivolous Herbert.

"Morris said the things happened so naturally," said his father, "that you might if you so wished attribute it to coincidence."

"Well, don't break into the money before I come back," said Herbert, as he rose from the table. "I'm afraid it'll turn you into a mean, avaricious man, and we shall have to disown you."

His mother laughed, and following him to the door, watched him down the road, and returning to the breakfast table, was very happy at the expense of her husband's credulity. All of which did not prevent her from scurrying to the door at the postman's knock, nor prevent her from referring somewhat shortly to retired sergeant-majors of bibulous habits when she found that the post brought a tailor's bill.

"Herbert will have some more of his funny remarks, I expect, when he comes home," she said, as they sat at dinner.

"I dare say," said Mr. White, pouring himself out some beer; "but for all that, the thing moved in my hand; that I'll swear to."

"You thought it did," said the old lady soothingly.

"I say it did," replied the other. "There was no thought about it; I had just—What's the matter?"

His wife made no reply. She was watching the mysterious movements of a man outside, who, peering in an undecided fashion at the house, appeared to be trying to make up his mind to enter. In mental connection with the two hundred pounds, she noticed that the stranger was well dressed and wore a silk hat of glossy newness. Three times he paused at the gate, and then walked on again. The fourth time he stood with his hand upon it, and then with sudden resolution flung it open and walked up the path. Mrs. White at the same moment placed her hands behind her, and hurriedly unfastening the strings of her apron, put that useful article of apparel beneath the cushion of her chair.

She brought the stranger, who seemed ill at ease, into the room. He gazed at her furtively, and listened in a preoccupied fashion as the old lady apologized for the appearance of the room, and her husband's coat, a garment which he usually reserved for the garden. She then waited as patiently as her sex would permit, for him to broach his business, but he was at first strangely silent.

"I—was asked to call," he said at last, and stooped and picked a piece of cotton from his trousers. "I come from Maw and Meggins."

The old lady started. "Is anything the matter?" she asked breathlessly. "Has anything happened to Herbert? What is it? What is it?"

Her husband interposed. "There, there, mother," he said hastily. "Sit down, and don't jump to conclusions. You've not brought bad news, I'm sure, sir" and he eyed the other wistfully.

"I'm sorry—" began the visitor.

"Is he hurt?" demanded the mother.

The visitor bowed in assent. "Badly hurt," he said quietly, "but he is not in any pain."

"Oh, thank God!" said the old woman, clasping her hands. "Thank God for that! Thank—"

She broke off suddenly as the sinister meaning of the assurance dawned upon her and she saw the awful confirmation of her fears in the other's averted face. She caught her breath, and turning to her slower-witted husband, laid her trembling old hand upon his. There was a long silence.

"He was caught in the machinery," said the visitor at length, in a low voice.

"Caught in the machinery," repeated Mr. White, in a dazed fashion, "yes."

He sat staring blankly out at the window, and taking his wife's hand between his own, pressed it as he had been wont to do in their old courting days nearly forty years before.

"He was the only one left to us," he said, turning gently to the visitor. "It is hard."

The other coughed, and rising, walked slowly to the window. "The firm wished me to convey their sincere sympathy with you in your great loss," he said, without looking round. "I beg that you will understand I am only their servant and merely obeying orders."

There was no reply; the old woman's face was white, her eyes staring, and her breath inaudible; on the husband's face was a look such as his friend the sergeant might have carried into his first action.

"I was to say that Maw and Meggins disclaim all responsibility," continued the other. "They admit no liability at all, but in consideration of your son's services they wish to present you with a certain sum as compensation."

Mr. White dropped his wife's hand, and rising to his feet, gazed with a look of horror at his visitor. His dry lips shaped the words, "How much?"

"Two hundred pounds," was the answer.

Unconscious of his wife's shriek, the old man smiled faintly, put out his hands like a sightless man, and dropped, a senseless heap, to the floor.

III

In the huge new cemetery, some two miles distant, the old people buried their dead, and came back to a house steeped in shadow and silence. It was all over so quickly that at first they could hardly realize it, and remained in a state of expectation as though of something else to happen—something else which was to lighten this load, too heavy for old hearts to bear.

But the days passed, and expectation gave place to resignation—the hopeless resignation of the old, sometimes miscalled, apathy. Sometimes they hardly exchanged a word, for now they had nothing to talk about, and their days were long to weariness.

It was about a week after that that the old man, waking suddenly in the night, stretched out his hand and found himself alone. The room was in darkness, and the sound of subdued weeping came from the window. He raised himself in bed and listened.

"Come back," he said tenderly. "You will be cold."

"It is colder for my son," said the old woman, and wept afresh.

The sound of her sobs died away on his ears. The bed was warm, and his eyes heavy with sleep. He dozed fitfully, and then slept until a sudden wild cry from his wife awoke him with a start.

"The paw!" she cried wildly. "The monkey's paw!"

He started up in alarm. "Where? Where is it? What's the matter?"

She came stumbling across the room toward him. "I want it," she said quietly. "You've not destroyed it?"

"It's in the parlour, on the bracket," he replied, marvelling. "Why?"

She cried and laughed together, and bending over, kissed his cheek.

"I only just thought of it," she said hysterically. "Why didn't I think of it before? Why didn't you think of it?"

"Think of what?" he questioned.

"The other two wishes," she replied rapidly. "We've only had one."

"Was not that enough?" he demanded fiercely.

"No," she cried, triumphantly; "we'll have one more. Go down and get it quickly, and wish our boy alive again."

The man sat up in bed and flung the bedclothes from his quaking limbs. "Good God, you are mad!" he cried aghast.

"Get it," she panted; "get it quickly, and wish—Oh, my boy, my boy!"

Her husband struck a match and lit the candle. "Get back to bed," he said, unsteadily. "You don't know what you are saying."

"We had the first wish granted," said the old woman, feverishly; "why not the second."

"A coincidence," stammered the old man.

"Go and get it and wish," cried the old woman, quivering with excitement.

The old man turned and regarded her, and his voice shook. "He has been dead ten days, and besides he—I would not tell you else, but—I could only recognize him by his clothing. If he was too terrible for you to see then, how now?"

"Bring him back," cried the old woman, and dragged him toward the door. "Do you think I fear the child I have nursed?"

He went down in the darkness, and felt his way to the parlour, and then to the mantelpiece. The talisman was in its place, and a horrible fear that the unspoken wish might bring his mutilated son before him ere he could escape from the room seized upon him, and he caught his breath as he found that he had lost the direction of the door. His brow cold with sweat, he felt his way round the table, and groped along the wall until he found himself in the small passage with the unwholesome thing in his hand.

Even his wife's face seemed changed as he entered the room. It was white and expectant, and to his fears seemed to have an unnatural look upon it. He was afraid of her.

"Wish!" she cried, in a strong voice.

"It is foolish and wicked," he faltered.

"Wish!" repeated his wife.

He raised his hand. "I wish my son alive again."

The talisman fell to the floor, and he regarded it fearfully. Then he sank trembling into a chair as the old woman, with burning eyes, walked to the window and raised the blind.

He sat until he was chilled with the cold, glancing occasionally at the figure of the old woman peering through the window. The candle end, which had burnt below the rim of the china candlestick, was throwing pulsating shadows on the ceiling and walls, until, with a flicker larger than the rest, it expired. The old man, with an unspeakable sense of relief at the failure of the talisman, crept back to his bed, and a minute or two afterward the old woman came silently and apathetically beside him.

Neither spoke, but both lay silently listening to the ticking of the clock. A stair creaked, and a squeaky mouse scurried noisily through the wall. The darkness was oppressive, and after lying for some time screwing up his courage, the husband took the box of matches, and striking one, went downstairs for a candle.

At the foot of the stairs the match went out, and he paused to strike another, and at the same moment a knock, so quiet and stealthy as to be scarcely audible, sounded on the front door.

The matches fell from his hand. He stood motionless, his breath suspended until the knock was repeated. Then he turned and fled swiftly back to his room, and closed the door behind him. A third knock sounded through the house.

"What's that?" cried the old woman, starting up.

"A rat," said the old man, in shaking tones—"a rat. It passed me on the stairs."

His wife sat up in bed listening. A loud knock resounded through the house.

"It's Herbert!" she screamed. "It's Herbert!"

She ran to the door, but her husband was before her, and catching her by the arm, held her tightly.

"What are you going to do?" he whispered hoarsely.

"It's my boy; it's Herbert!" she cried, struggling mechanically. "I forgot it was two miles away. What are you holding me for? Let go. I must open the door."

"For God's sake, don't let it in," cried the old man trembling.

"You're afraid of your own son," she cried, struggling. "Let me go. I'm coming, Herbert; I'm coming."

There was another knock, and another. The old woman with a sudden wrench broke free and ran from the room. Her husband followed to the landing, and called after her appealingly as she hurried downstairs. He heard the chain rattle back and the bottom bolt drawn slowly and stiffly from the socket. Then the old woman's voice, strained and panting.

"The bolt," she cried loudly. "Come down. I can't reach it."

But her husband was on his hands and knees groping wildly on the floor in search of the paw. If he could only find it before the thing outside got in. A perfect fusillade of knocks reverberated through the house, and he heard the scraping of a chair as his wife put it down in the passage against the door. He heard the creaking of the bolt as it came slowly back, and at the same moment he found the monkey's paw, and frantically breathed his third and last wish.

The knocking ceased suddenly, although the echoes of it were still in the house. He heard the chair drawn back and the door opened. A cold wind rushed up the staircase, and a long loud wail of disappointment and misery from his wife gave him courage to run down to her side, and then to the gate beyond. The street lamp, flickering opposite, shone on a quiet and deserted road.

A3

Consequences and Implications

Explain the implications and consequences of choices we make and how those affect others. Link your insights from the story to a personal situation.

A2

Cause and Effect

Why did the sergeant-major present the monkey paw to the family when he knew it was evil?

A1

Sequencing

What are the five most critical events in the story? Sequence them.

THE MONKEY'S PAW

Generalizations

B3

Write three generalizations about this story that show the relationship between greed and happiness.

Classifications

B2

Detail the events of the story that show greed and that show happiness. Create a T-chart to categorize your ideas.

Details

B1

How would you describe the family in this story, based on the details provided?

THE MONKEY'S PAW

Creative Synthesis

D3

Is this story a fairy tale? Why or why not? Write a persuasive
essay to convince someone of your opinion.

Summarizing

D2

Create two columns on a piece of paper. In Column 1, write the elements
of a fairy tale from D1. In Column 2, summarize events from the story
that match the elements of a fairy tale from the first column. Do you
have a match from the story for every element? Why or why not?

Paraphrasing

D1

What are the basic elements of a fairy tale?
Describe them in your own words.

THE MONKEY'S PAW

The Diamond Necklace

By Guy de Maupassant

The girl was one of those pretty and charming young creatures who sometimes are born, as if by a slip of fate, into a family of clerks. She had no dowry, no expectations, no way of being known, understood, loved, married by any rich and distinguished man; so she let herself be married to a little clerk of the Ministry of Public Instruction.

She dressed plainly because she could not dress well, but she was unhappy as if she had really fallen from a higher station; since with women there is neither caste nor rank, for beauty, grace and charm take the place of family and birth. Natural ingenuity, instinct for what is elegant, a supple mind are their sole hierarchy, and often make of women of the people the equals of the very greatest ladies.

Mathilde suffered ceaselessly, feeling herself born to enjoy all delicacies and all luxuries. She was distressed at the poverty of her dwelling, at the bareness of the walls, at the shabby chairs, the ugliness of the curtains. All those things, of which another woman of her rank would never even have been conscious, tortured her and made her angry. The sight of the little Breton peasant who did her humble housework aroused in her despairing regrets and bewildering dreams. She thought of silent antechambers hung with Oriental tapestry, illumined by tall bronze candelabra, and of two great footmen in knee breeches who sleep in the big armchairs, made drowsy by the oppressive heat of the stove. She thought of long reception halls hung with ancient silk, of the dainty cabinets containing priceless curiosities and of the little coquettish perfumed reception rooms made for chatting at five o'clock with intimate friends, with men famous and sought after, whom all women envy and whose attention they all desire.

When she sat down to dinner, before the round table covered with a tablecloth in use three days, opposite her husband, who uncovered the soup tureen and declared with a delighted air, "Ah, the good soup! I don't know anything better than that," she thought of dainty dinners, of shining silverware, of tapestry that peopled the walls with ancient personages and with strange birds flying in the midst of a fairy forest; and she thought of delicious dishes served on marvelous plates and of the whispered gallantries to which you listen with a sphinxlike smile while you are eating the pink meat of a trout or the wings of a quail.

She had no gowns, no jewels, nothing. And she loved nothing but that. She felt made for that. She would have liked so much to please, to be envied, to be charming, to be sought after.

She had a friend, a former schoolmate at the convent, who was rich, and whom she did not like to go to see any more because she felt so sad when she came home.

But one evening her husband reached home with a triumphant air and holding a large envelope in his hand.

"There," said he, "there is something for you."

She tore the paper quickly and drew out a printed card which bore these words:

> The Minister of Public Instruction and Madame Georges Ramponneau request the honor of M. and Madame Loisel's company at the palace of the Ministry on Monday evening, January 18th.

Instead of being delighted, as her husband had hoped, she threw the invitation on the table crossly, muttering:

"What do you wish me to do with that?"

"Why, my dear, I thought you would be glad. You never go out, and this is such a fine opportunity. I had great trouble to get it. Every one wants to go; it is very select, and they are not giving many invitations to clerks. The whole official world will be there."

She looked at him with an irritated glance and said impatiently:

"And what do you wish me to put on my back?"

He had not thought of that. He stammered:

"Why, the gown you go to the theatre in. It looks very well to me."

He stopped, distracted, seeing that his wife was weeping. Two great tears ran slowly from the corners of her eyes toward the corners of her mouth.

"What's the matter? What's the matter?" he answered.

By a violent effort she conquered her grief and replied in a calm voice, while she wiped her wet cheeks:

"Nothing. Only I have no gown, and, therefore, I can't go to this ball. Give your card to some colleague whose wife is better equipped than I am."

He was in despair. He resumed:

"Come, let us see, Mathilde. How much would it cost, a suitable gown, which you could use on other occasions—something very simple?"

She reflected several seconds, making her calculations and wondering also what sum she could ask without drawing on herself an immediate refusal and a frightened exclamation from the economical clerk.

Finally she replied hesitating:

"I don't know exactly, but I think I could manage it with four hundred francs."

He grew a little pale, because he was laying aside just that amount to buy a gun and treat himself to a little shooting next summer on the plain of Nanterre, with several friends who went to shoot larks there of a Sunday.

But he said:

"Very well. I will give you four hundred francs. And try to have a pretty gown."

The day of the ball drew near and Madame Loisel seemed sad, uneasy, anxious. Her frock was ready, however. Her husband said to her one evening:

"What is the matter? Come, you have seemed very queer these last three days."

And she answered:

"It annoys me not to have a single piece of jewelry, not a single ornament, nothing to put on. I shall look poverty-stricken. I would almost rather not go at all."

"You might wear natural flowers," said her husband. "They're very stylish at this time of year. For ten francs you can get two or three magnificent roses."

She was not convinced.

"No; there's nothing more humiliating than to look poor among other women who are rich."

"How stupid you are!" her husband cried. "Go look up your friend, Madame Forestier, and ask her to lend you some jewels. You're intimate enough with her to do that."

She uttered a cry of joy:

"True! I never thought of it."

The next day she went to her friend and told her of her distress.

Madame Forestier went to a wardrobe with a mirror, took out a large jewel box, brought it back, opened it and said to Madame Loisel:

"Choose, my dear."

She saw first some bracelets, then a pearl necklace, then a Venetian gold cross set with precious stones, of admirable workmanship. She tried on the ornaments before the mirror, hesitated and could not make up her mind to part with them, to give them back. She kept asking:

"Haven't you any more?"

"Why, yes. Look further; I don't know what you like."

Suddenly she discovered, in a black satin box, a superb diamond necklace, and her heart throbbed with an immoderate desire. Her hands trembled as she took it. She fastened it round her throat, outside her high-necked waist, and was lost in ecstasy at her reflection in the mirror.

Then she asked, hesitating, filled with anxious doubt:

"Will you lend me this, only this?"

"Why, yes, certainly."

She threw her arms round her friend's neck, kissed her passionately, then fled with her treasure.

The night of the ball arrived. Madame Loisel was a great success. She was prettier than any other woman present, elegant, graceful, smiling and wild with joy. All the men looked at her, asked her name, sought to be introduced. All the attaches of the Cabinet wished to waltz with her. She was remarked by the minister himself.

She danced with rapture, with passion, intoxicated by pleasure, forgetting all in the triumph of her beauty, in the glory of her success, in a sort of cloud of happiness comprised of all this homage, admiration, these awakened desires and of that sense of triumph which is so sweet to woman's heart.

She left the ball about four o'clock in the morning. Her husband had been sleeping since midnight in a little deserted anteroom with three other gentlemen whose wives were enjoying the ball.

He threw over her shoulders the wraps he had brought, the modest wraps of common life, the poverty of which contrasted with the elegance of the ball dress. She felt this and wished to escape so as not to be remarked by the other women, who were enveloping themselves in costly furs.

Loisel held her back, saying: "Wait a bit. You will catch cold outside. I will call a cab."

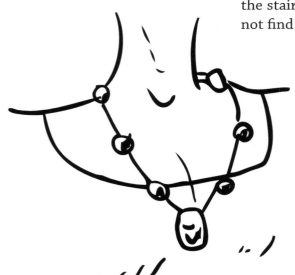

But she did not listen to him and rapidly descended the stairs. When they reached the street they could not find a carriage and began to look for one, shouting after the cabmen passing at a distance.

They went toward the Seine in despair, shivering with cold. At last they found on the quay one of those ancient night cabs which, as though they were ashamed to show their shabbiness during the day, are never seen round Paris until after dark.

It took them to their dwelling in the Rue des Martyrs, and sadly they mounted the stairs to their flat. All was ended for her.

As to him, he reflected that he must be at the ministry at ten o'clock that morning.

She removed her wraps before the glass so as to see herself once more in all her glory. But suddenly she uttered a cry. She no longer had the necklace around her neck!

"What is the matter with you?" demanded her husband, already half undressed.

She turned distractedly toward him.

"I have—I have—I've lost Madame Forestier's necklace," she cried.

He stood up, bewildered.

"What!—how? Impossible!"

They looked among the folds of her skirt, of her cloak, in her pockets, everywhere, but did not find it.

"You're sure you had it on when you left the ball?" he asked.

"Yes, I felt it in the vestibule of the minister's house."

"But if you had lost it in the street we should have heard it fall. It must be in the cab."

"Yes, probably. Did you take his number?"

"No. And you—didn't you notice it?"

"No."

They looked, thunderstruck, at each other. At last Loisel put on his clothes.

"I shall go back on foot," said he, "over the whole route, to see whether I can find it."

He went out. She sat waiting on a chair in her ball dress, without strength to go to bed, overwhelmed, without any fire, without a thought.

Her husband returned about seven o'clock. He had found nothing.

He went to police headquarters, to the newspaper offices to offer a reward; he went to the cab companies—everywhere, in fact, whither he was urged by the least spark of hope.

She waited all day, in the same condition of mad fear before this terrible calamity.

Loisel returned at night with a hollow, pale face. He had discovered nothing.

"You must write to your friend," said he, "that you have broken the clasp of her necklace and that you are having it mended. That will give us time to turn round."

She wrote at his dictation.

At the end of a week they had lost all hope. Loisel, who had aged five years, declared:

"We must consider how to replace that ornament."

The next day they took the box that had contained it and went to the jeweler whose name was found within. He consulted his books.

"It was not I, madame, who sold that necklace; I must simply have furnished the case."

Then they went from jeweler to jeweler, searching for a necklace like the other, trying to recall it, both sick with chagrin and grief.

They found, in a shop at the Palais Royal, a string of diamonds that seemed to them exactly like the one they had lost. It was worth forty thousand francs. They could have it for thirty-six.

So they begged the jeweler not to sell it for three days yet. And they made a bargain that he should buy it back for thirty-four thousand francs, in case they should find the lost necklace before the end of February.

Loisel possessed eighteen thousand francs which his father had left him. He would borrow the rest.

He did borrow, asking a thousand francs of one, five hundred of another, five louis here, three louis there. He gave notes, took up ruinous obligations, dealt with usurers and all the race of lenders. He compromised all the rest of his life, risked signing a note without even knowing whether he could meet it; and, frightened by the trouble yet to come, by the black misery that was about to fall upon him, by the prospect of all the physical privations and moral tortures that he was to suffer, he went to get the new necklace, laying upon the jeweler's counter thirty-six thousand francs.

When Madame Loisel took back the necklace Madame Forestier said to her with a chilly manner:

"You should have returned it sooner; I might have needed it."

She did not open the case, as her friend had so much feared. If she had detected the substitution, what would she have thought, what would she have said? Would she not have taken Madame Loisel for a thief?

Thereafter Madame Loisel knew the horrible existence of the needy. She bore her part, however, with sudden heroism. That dreadful debt must be paid. She would pay it. They dismissed their servant; they changed their lodgings; they rented a garret under the roof.

She came to know what heavy housework meant and the odious cares of the kitchen. She washed the dishes, using her dainty fingers and rosy nails on greasy pots and pans. She washed the soiled linen, the shirts and the dishcloths, which she dried upon a line; she carried the slops down to the street every morning and carried up the water, stopping for breath at every landing. And dressed like a woman of the people, she went to the fruiterer, the grocer, the butcher, a basket on her arm, bargaining, meeting with impertinence, defending her miserable money, sou by sou.

Every month they had to meet some notes, renew others, obtain more time.

Her husband worked evenings, making up a tradesman's accounts, and late at night he often copied manuscript for five sous a page.

This life lasted ten years.

At the end of ten years they had paid everything, everything, with the rates of usury and the accumulations of the compound interest.

Madame Loisel looked old now. She had become the woman of impoverished households—strong and hard and rough. With frowsy hair, skirts askew and red hands, she talked loud while washing the floor with great swishes of water. But sometimes, when her husband was at the office, she sat down near the window and she thought of that gay evening of long ago, of that ball where she had been so beautiful and so admired.

What would have happened if she had not lost that necklace? Who knows? Who knows? How strange and changeful is life! How small a thing is needed to make or ruin us!

But one Sunday, having gone to take a walk in the Champs Elysees to refresh herself after the labors of the week, she suddenly perceived a woman who was leading a child. It was Madame Forestier, still young, still beautiful, still charming.

Madame Loisel felt moved. Should she speak to her? Yes, certainly. And now that she had paid, she would tell her all about it. Why not?

She went up.

"Good-day, Jeanne."

The other, astonished to be familiarly addressed by this plain good-wife, did not recognize her at all and stammered:

"But—madame!—I do not know—You must have mistaken."

"No. I am Mathilde Loisel."

Her friend uttered a cry.

"Oh, my poor Mathilde! How you are changed!"

"Yes, I have had a pretty hard life, since I last saw you, and great poverty—and that because of you!"

"Of me! How so?"

"Do you remember that diamond necklace you lent me to wear at the ministerial ball?"

"Yes. Well?"

"Well, I lost it."

"What do you mean? You brought it back."

"I brought you back another exactly like it. And it has taken us ten years to pay for it. You can understand that it was not easy for us, for us who had nothing. At last it is ended, and I am very glad."

Madame Forestier had stopped.

"You say that you bought a necklace of diamonds to replace mine?"

"Yes. You never noticed it, then! They were very similar."

And she smiled with a joy that was at once proud and ingenuous.

Madame Forestier, deeply moved, took her hands.

"Oh, my poor Mathilde! Why, my necklace was paste! It was worth at most only five hundred francs!"

Consequences and Implications

A3

What are the consequences of never being happy with what you have, according to de Maupassant?

Cause and Effect

A2

What are the cause-and-effect relationships in this story? Which one is most significant? Why?

Sequencing

A1

Make an outline of the most important events of the story. Explain why the events you listed are the most important.

THE DIAMOND NECKLACE

Main Idea, Theme, or Concept

C3

What message do you think de Maupassant wanted to convey? Why? How are the themes of love and beauty used in the story by de Maupassant?

Inference

C2

What does this story suggest about friendship? About satisfaction? About beauty? What can we infer about the meaning of the story from its ending?

Literary Elements

C1

How is the characterization of Mathilde important to the meaning of this story? What qualities does she possess?

THE DIAMOND NECKLACE

Using Emotion

E3

How did emotion drive the telling of the story? Explain your answer using evidence from the text.

Expressing Emotion

E2

When should you be satisfied with what you have, and when should you strive for something better? How are your thoughts similar to or different from the characters' in the story?

Understanding Emotion

E1

How did you feel at the end of the story? Why?

The Celebrated Jumping Frog of Calaveras County

By Mark Twain

Mr. A. Ward,

Dear Sir:—Well, I called on good-natured, garrulous old Simon Wheeler, and inquired after your friend, Leonidas W. Smiley, as you requested me to do, and I hereunto append the result. If you can get any information out of it you are cordially welcome to it. I have a lurking suspicion that your Leonidas W. Smiley is a myth—that you never knew such a personage, and that you only conjectured that if I asked old Wheeler about him it would remind him of his infamous *Jim* Smiley, and he would go to work and bore me nearly to death with some infernal reminiscence of him as long and tedious as it should be useless to me. If that was your design, Mr. Ward, it will gratify you to know that it succeeded.

I found Simon Wheeler dozing comfortably by the bar-room stove of the old, dilapidated tavern in the ancient mining camp of Boomerang, and I noticed that he was fat and bald-headed, and had an expression of winning gentleness and simplicity upon his tranquil countenance. He roused up and gave me good-day. I told him a friend of mine had commissioned me to make some inquiries about a cherished companion of his boyhood named Leonidas W. Smiley—Rev. Leonidas W. Smiley—a young minister of the Gospel, who he had heard was at one time a resident of this village of Boomerang. I added that if Mr. Wheeler could tell me any thing about this Rev. Leonidas W. Smiley, I would feel under many obligations to him.

Simon Wheeler backed me into a corner and blockaded me there with his chair—and then sat me down and reeled off the monotonous narrative which follows this paragraph. He never smiled, he never frowned, he never changed his voice from the gentle-flowing key to which he tuned the initial sentence, he never betrayed the slightest suspicion of enthusiasm—but all through the interminable narrative there ran a vein of impressive earnestness and sincerity, which showed me plainly that, so far from his imagining that there was any thing ridiculous or funny about his story, he regarded it as a really important matter, and admired its two heroes as men of transcendent genius in finesse. To me, the spectacle of a man drifting serenely along through such a queer yarn without ever smiling was exquisitely absurd. As I said before, I asked him to tell me what he knew of

Rev. Leonidas W. Smiley, and he replied as follows. I let him go on in his own way, and never interrupted him once:

There was a feller here once by the name of *Jim* Smiley, in the winter of '49—or maybe it was the spring of '50—I don't recollect exactly, somehow, though what makes me think it was one or the other is because I remember the big flume wasn't finished when he first came to the camp; but any way, he was the curiosest man about always betting on any thing that turned up you ever see, if he could get any body to bet on the other side, and if he couldn't he'd change sides—any way that suited the other man would suit *him*—any way just so's he got a bet, *he* was satisfied. But still, he was lucky—uncommon lucky; he most always come out winner. He was always ready and laying for a chance; there couldn't be no solitry thing mentioned but that feller'd offer to bet on it—and take any side you please, as I was just telling you. If there was a horse-race, you'd find him flush, or you'd find him busted at the end of it; if there was a dog-fight, he'd bet on it; if there was a cat-fight, he'd bet on it; if there was a chicken-fight, he'd bet on it; why, if there was two birds setting on a fence, he would bet you which one would fly first—or if there was a camp-meeting, he would be there reglar, to bet on Parson Walker, which he judged to be the best exhorter about here, and so he was, too, and a good man. If he even seen a straddle-bug start to go any wheres, he would bet you how long it would take him to get wher-ever he was going to, and if you took him up, he would foller that straddle-bug to Mexico but what he would find out where he was bound for and how long he was on the road. Lots of the boys here has seen that Smiley, and can tell you about him. Why, it never made no difference to *him*—he would bet on *anything*—the dangdest feller. Parson Walker's wife laid very sick, once, for a good while, and it seemed as if they warn't going to save her; but one morning he come in, and Smiley asked him how she was, and he said she was considerable better— thank the Lord for his inf'nit mercy—and coming on so smart that, with the blessing of Providence, she'd get well yet—and Smiley, before he thought, says, "Well, I'll resk two-and-a-half that she don't, anyway."

Thish-yer Smiley had a mare—the boys called her the fifteen-minute nag, but that was only in fun, you know, because, of course, she was faster than that—and he used to win money on that horse, for all she was so slow and always had the asthma, or the distemper, or the consumption, or something of that kind. They used to give her two or three hundred yards' start, and then pass her under way; but always at the fag-end of the race she'd get excited and desperate-like, and come cavorting and straddling up, and scattering her legs around limber, sometimes in the air, and sometimes out to one side amongst the fences, and kicking up m-o-r-e dust, and raising m-o-r-e racket with her coughing and sneezing and blowing her nose—and always fetch up at the stand just about a neck ahead, as near as you could cipher it down.

And he had a little small bull pup, that to look at him you'd think he warn't worth a cent, but to set around and look ornery, and lay for a chance to steal something. But as soon as money was up on him, he was a different dog—his underjaw'd begin to stick out like the fo'castle of a steamboat, and his teeth would uncover, and shine savage like the furnaces. And a dog might tackle him, and bully-rag him, and bite him, and throw him over his shoulder two or three times, and Andrew Jackson—which was the name of the pup—Andrew Jackson would never let on but what he was satisfied, and hadn't expected nothing else—and the bets being doubled and doubled on the other side all the time, till the money was all up—and then all of a sudden he would grab that other dog jest by the j'int of his hind leg and freeze to it—not chaw, you understand, but only jest grip and hang on till they thronged up the sponge, if it was a year. Smiley always come out winner on that pup, till he harnessed a dog once that didn't have no hind legs, because they'd been sawed off in a circular saw, and when the thing had gone along far enough, and the money was all up, and he come to make a snatch for his pet holt, he saw in a minute how he'd been imposed on, and how the other dog had him in the door, so to speak, and he 'peared surprised, and then he looked sorter discouraged-like, and didn't try no more to win the fight, and so he got shucked out bad. He give Smiley a look, as much as to say his heart was broke, and it was *his* fault, for putting up a dog that hadn't no hind legs for him to take holt of, which was his main dependence in a fight, and then he limped off a piece and laid down and died. It was a good pup, was that Andrew Jackson, and would have made a name for hisself if he'd lived, for the stuff was in him, and he had genius—I know it, because he hadn't had no opportunities to speak of, and it don't stand to reason that a dog could make such a fight as he could under them circumstances, if he hadn't no talent. It always makes me feel sorry when I think of that last fight of his'n, and the way it turned out.

Well, thish-yer Smiley had rat-tarriers, and chicken cocks, and tom-cats, and all of them kind of things, till you couldn't rest, and you couldn't fetch nothing for him to bet on but he'd match you. He ketched a frog one day, and took him home, and said he cal'klated to edercate him; and so he never done nothing for three months but set in his back yard and learn that frog to jump. And you bet you he *did* learn him, too. He'd give him a little hunch behind, and the next minute you'd see that frog whirling in the air like a doughnut—see him turn one summerset, or may be a couple, if he got a good start, and come down flat-footed and all right, like a cat. He got him up so in the matter of ketching flies, and kept him in practice so constant, that he'd nail a fly every time as far as he could see him. Smiley said all a frog wanted was education, and he could do most anything—and I believe him. Why, I've seen him set Dan'l Webster down here on this floor—Dan'l Webster was the name of the frog—and sing out, "Flies, Dan'l, flies!" and quicker'n you could wink, he'd spring straight up, and snake a fly off'n the counter there, and flop down on the floor again as solid as a gob of mud, and fall to scratching the side of his head with his hind foot as indifferent as if he hadn't no idea he'd been doin' any more'n any frog might do. You never see a frog so modest and straightfor'ard as he was, for all he was so gifted. And when it come to fair-and-square jumping on a dead level, he could get over more ground at one straddle than any animal of his breed you ever see. Jumping on a dead level was his strong suit, you understand, and when it come to that, Smiley would ante up money on him as long as he had a red. Smiley was monstrous proud of his frog, and well he might be, for fellers that had traveled and ben everywheres, all said he laid over any frog that *ever* they see.

Well, Smiley kept the beast in a little lattice box, and he used to fetch him down town sometimes and lay for a bet. One day a feller—a stranger in the camp, he was—come across him with his box, and says:

"What might it be that you've got in the box?"

And Smiley says, sorter indifferent like, "It might be a parrot, or it might be a canary, may be, but it ain't—it's only just a frog."

And the feller took it, and looked at it careful, and turned it round this way and that, and says, "H'm—so 'tis. Well, what's *he* good for?"

"Well," Smiley says, easy and careless, "He's good enough for *one* thing, I should judge—he can out-jump ary frog in Calaveras county."

The feller took the box again, and took another long, particular look, and give it back to Smiley, and says, very deliberate, "Well—I don't see no p'ints about that frog that's any better'n any other frog."

"Maybe you don't," Smiley says. "Maybe you understand frogs, and maybe you don't understand 'em; maybe you've had experience, and maybe you ain't only a amature, as it were. Anyways, I've got *my* opinion, and I'll resk forty dollars that he can outjump any frog in Calaveras county."

And the feller studied a minute, and then says, kinder sad, like, "Well, I'm only a stranger here, and I ain't got no frog—but if I had a frog, I'd bet you."

And then Smiley says, "That's all right—that's all right—if you'll hold my box a minute, I'll go and get you a frog." And so the feller took the box, and put up his forty dollars along with Smiley's, and set down to wait.

So he set there a good while thinking and thinking to hisself, and then he got the frog out and prized his mouth open and took a tea-spoon and filled him full of quail shot—filled him pretty near up to his chin—and set him on the floor. Smiley he went to the swamp and slopped around in the mud for a long time, and finally he ketched a frog, and fetched him in, and give him to this feller, and says:

"Now if you're ready, set him alongside of Dan'l, with his fore-paws just even with Dan'l's, and I'll give the word." Then he says, "One—two—three—jump!" and him and the feller touched up the frogs from behind, and the new frog hopped off, but Dan'l give a heave, and hysted up his shoulders—so—like a Frenchman, but it wasn't no use—he couldn't budge; he was planted as solid as an anvil, and he couldn't no more stir than if he was anchored out. Smiley was a good deal surprised, and he was disgusted too, but he didn't have no idea what the matter was, of course.

The feller took the money and started away; and when he was going out at the door, he sorter jerked his thumb over his shoulders—this way—at Dan'l, and says again, very deliberate, "Well, *I* don't see no p'ints about that frog that's any better'n any other frog."

Smiley he stood scratching his head and looking down at Dan'l a long time, and at last he says, "I do wonder what in the nation that frog throw'd off for—I wonder if there ain't something the matter with him—he 'pears to look mighty baggy, somehow"—and he ketched Dan'l by the nap of the neck, and lifted him up and says, "Why, blame my cats, if he don't weigh five pound!"—and turned him upside down, and he belched out a double-handful of shot. And then he see how it was, and he was the maddest man—he set the frog down and took out after that feller, but he never ketched him. And—

Here Simon Wheeler heard his name called from the front yard, and got up to go and see what was wanted. And turning to me as he moved away, he said: "Just set where you are, stranger, and rest easy—I an't going to be gone a second."

But, by your leave, I did not think that a continuation of the history of the enterprising vagabond Jim

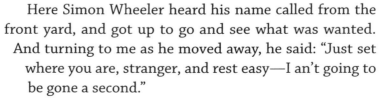

Smiley would be likely to afford me much information concerning the Rev. Leonidas W. Smiley, and so I started away.

At the door I met the sociable Wheeler returning, and he button-holed me and recommenced:

"Well, thish-yer Smiley had a yeller one-eyed cow that didn't have no tail, only jest a short stump like a bannanner, and"

"O, curse Smiley and his afflicted cow!" I muttered, good-naturedly, and bidding the old gentleman good-day, I departed.

Consequences and Implications

What are the implications of the names of the characters in the story? How do those names add to the story's impact?

Cause and Effect

Examine the effects of Twain's use of language on the story. Make a chart with the following two categories: Story Quote and Effect on the Reader. Complete the chart using evidence from the text. An example has been started for you.

Story Quote	Effect on the Reader
"If there was a . . . he'd bet on it." (Repeated several times.)	Repetition emphasizes importance

Sequencing

Sequence the events that led up to the contest.

THE CELEBRATED JUMPING FROG OF CALAVERAS COUNTY

Main Idea, Theme, or Concept

C3

You may have heard the saying "Truth is stranger than fiction." How does Twain keep his reader engaged in the story to make it believable?

Inference

C2

How does Twain use hyperbole and humor to create an entertaining story?

Literary Elements

C1

Find examples of hyperbole and humor in this story. Highlight them in the text.

THE CELEBRATED JUMPING FROG OF CALAVERAS COUNTY

Creative Synthesis

D3

Many writers are successful because they are able to use events in their own lives and adapt them to fictional situations. Write a humorous tale by exaggerating an event from your life.

THE CELEBRATED JUMPING FROG OF CALAVERAS COUNTY

Summarizing

D2

Summarize the purpose of this story.

Paraphrasing

D1

Paraphrase the ending of this story and its significance.

The Lottery Ticket

By Anton Chekhov

Ivan Dmitritch, a middle-class man who lived with his family on an income of twelve hundred a year and was very well satisfied with his lot, sat down on the sofa after supper and began reading the newspaper.

"I forgot to look at the newspaper today," his wife said to him as she cleared the table. "Look and see whether the list of drawings is there."

"Yes, it is," said Ivan Dmitritch; "but hasn't your ticket lapsed?"

"No; I took the interest on Tuesday."

"What is the number?"

"Series 9,499, number 26."

"All right . . . we will look . . . 9,499 and 26."

Ivan Dmitritch had no faith in lottery luck, and would not, as a rule, have consented to look at the lists of winning numbers, but now, as he had nothing else to do and as the newspaper was before his eyes, he passed his finger downwards along the column of numbers. And immediately, as though in mockery of his skepticism, no further than the second line from the top, his eye was caught by the figure 9,499! Unable to believe his eyes, he hurriedly dropped the paper on his knees without looking to see the number of the ticket, and, just as though some one had given him a douche of cold water, he felt an agreeable chill in the pit of the stomach; tingling and terrible and sweet!

"Masha, 9,499 is there!" he said in a hollow voice.

His wife looked at his astonished and panic-stricken face, and realized that he was not joking.

"9,499?" she asked, turning pale and dropping the folded tablecloth on the table.

"Yes, yes . . . it really is there!"

"And the number of the ticket?"

"Oh, yes! There's the number of the ticket too. But stay . . . wait! No, I say! Anyway, the number of our series is there! Anyway, you understand. . . ."

Looking at his wife, Ivan Dmitritch gave a broad, senseless smile, like a baby when a bright object is shown it. His wife smiled too; it was as pleasant to her as to him that he only mentioned the series, and did not try to find out the number of the winning ticket. To torment and tantalize oneself with hopes of possible fortune is so sweet, so thrilling!

"It is our series," said Ivan Dmitritch, after a long silence. "So there is a probability that we have won. It's only a probability, but there it is!"

"Well, now look!"

"Wait a little. We have plenty of time to be disappointed. It's on the second line from the top, so the prize is seventy-five thousand. That's not money, but power, capital! And in a minute I shall look at the list, and there—26! Eh? I say, what if we really have won?"

The husband and wife began laughing and staring at one another in silence. The possibility of winning bewildered them; they could not have said, could not have dreamed, what they both needed that seventy-five thousand for, what they would buy, where they would go. They thought only of the figures 9,499 and 75,000 and pictured them in their imagination, while somehow they could not think of the happiness itself which was so possible.

Ivan Dmitritch, holding the paper in his hand, walked several times from corner to corner, and only when he had recovered from the first impression began dreaming a little.

"And if we have won," he said—"why, it will be a new life, it will be a transformation! The ticket is yours, but if it were mine I should, first of all, of course, spend twenty-five thousand on real property in the shape of an estate; ten thousand on immediate expenses, new furnishing . . . travelling . . . paying debts, and so on. . . . The other forty thousand I would put in the bank and get interest on it."

"Yes, an estate, that would be nice," said his wife, sitting down and dropping her hands in her lap.

"Somewhere in the Tula or Oryol provinces. . . . In the first place we shouldn't need a summer villa, and besides, it would always bring in an income."

And pictures came crowding on his imagination, each more gracious and poetical than the last. And in all these pictures he saw himself well-fed, serene, healthy, felt warm, even hot! Here, after eating a summer soup, cold as ice, he lay on his back on the burning sand close to a stream or in the garden under a lime-tree. . . . It is hot. . . . His little boy and girl are crawling about near him, digging in the sand or catching ladybirds in the grass. He dozes sweetly, thinking of nothing, and feeling all over that he need not go to the office today, tomorrow, or the day after. Or, tired of lying still, he goes to the hayfield, or to the forest for mushrooms, or watches the peasants catching fish with a net. When the sun sets he takes a towel and soap and saunters to the bathing-shed, where he undresses at his leisure, slowly rubs his bare chest with his hands, and goes into the water. And in the water, near the opaque soapy circles, little fish flit to and fro and green water-weeds nod their heads. After bathing there is tea with cream and milk rolls. . . . In the evening a walk or *vint* with the neighbours.

"Yes, it would be nice to buy an estate," said his wife, also dreaming, and from her face it was evident that she was enchanted by her thoughts.

Ivan Dmitritch pictured to himself autumn with its rains, its cold evenings, and its St. Martin's summer. At that season he would have to take longer walks about the garden and beside the river, so as to get thoroughly chilled, and then drink a big glass of vodka and eat a salted mushroom or a soused cucumber, and then—drink another. . . . The children would come running from the kitchen-garden, bringing a carrot and a radish smelling of fresh earth. . . . And then, he would lie stretched full length on the sofa, and in leisurely fashion turn over the pages of some illustrated magazine, or, covering his face with it and unbuttoning his waistcoat, give himself up to slumber.

The St. Martin's summer is followed by cloudy, gloomy weather. It rains day and night, the bare trees weep, the wind is damp and cold. The dogs, the horses, the fowls—all are wet, depressed, downcast. There is nowhere to walk; one can't go out for days together; one has to pace up and down the room, looking despondently at the grey window. It is dreary!

Ivan Dmitritch stopped and looked at his wife.

"I should go abroad, you know, Masha," he said.

And he began thinking how nice it would be in late autumn to go abroad somewhere to the South of France . . . to Italy . . . to India!

"I should certainly go abroad too," his wife said. "But look at the number of the ticket!"

"Wait, wait! . . ."

He walked about the room and went on thinking. It occurred to him: what if his wife really did go abroad? It is pleasant to travel alone, or in the society of light, careless women who live in the present, and not such as think and talk all the journey about nothing but their children, sigh, and tremble with dismay over every farthing. Ivan Dmitritch imagined his wife in the train with a multitude of parcels, baskets, and bags; she would be sighing over something, complaining that the train made her head ache, that she had spent so much money. . . . At the stations he would continually be having to run for boiling water, bread and butter. . . . She wouldn't have dinner because of its being too dear. . . .

"She would begrudge me every farthing," he thought, with a glance at his wife. "The lottery ticket is hers, not mine! Besides, what is the use of her going abroad? What does she want there? She would shut herself up in the hotel, and not let me out of her sight. . . . I know!"

And for the first time in his life his mind dwelt on the fact that his wife had grown elderly and plain, and that she was saturated through and through with the smell of cooking, while he was still young, fresh, and healthy, and might well have got married again.

"Of course, all that is silly nonsense," he thought; "but . . . why should she go abroad? What would she make of it? And yet she would go, of course. . . . I can fancy . . . In reality it is all one to her, whether it is Naples or Klin. She would only be in my way. I should be dependent upon her. I can fancy how, like a regular woman, she will lock the money up as soon as she gets it. . . . She will hide it from me. . . . She will look after her relations and grudge me every farthing."

Ivan Dmitritch thought of her relations. All those wretched brothers and sisters and aunts and uncles would come crawling about as soon as they heard of the winning ticket, would begin whining like beggars, and fawning upon them with oily, hypocritical smiles. Wretched, detestable people! If they were given anything, they would ask for more; while if they were refused, they would swear at them, slander them, and wish them every kind of misfortune.

Ivan Dmitritch remembered his own relations, and their faces, at which he had looked impartially in the past, struck him now as repulsive and hateful.

"They are such reptiles!" he thought.

And his wife's face, too, struck him as repulsive and hateful. Anger surged up in his heart against her, and he thought malignantly:

"She knows nothing about money, and so she is stingy. If she won it she would give me a hundred roubles, and put the rest away under lock and key."

And he looked at his wife, not with a smile now, but with hatred. She glanced at him too, and also with hatred and anger. She had her own daydreams, her own plans, her own reflections; she understood perfectly well what her husband's dreams were. She knew who would be the first to try and grab her winnings.

"It's very nice making daydreams at other people's expense!" is what her eyes expressed. "No, don't you dare!"

Her husband understood her look; hatred began stirring again in his breast, and in order to annoy his wife he glanced quickly, to spite her at the fourth page on the newspaper and read out triumphantly:

"Series 9,499, number 46! Not 26!"

Hatred and hope both disappeared at once, and it began immediately to seem to Ivan Dmitritch and his wife that their rooms were dark and small and low-pitched, that the supper they had been eating was not doing them good, but lying heavy on their stomachs, that the evenings were long and wearisome. . . .

"What the devil's the meaning of it?" said Ivan Dmitritch, beginning to be ill-humoured. "Wherever one steps there are bits of paper under one's feet, crumbs, husks. The rooms are never swept! One is simply forced to go out. Damnation take my soul entirely! I shall go and hang myself on the first aspen-tree!"

Generalizations

B3

Write three generalizations about happiness, based on your examples. How do these generalizations hold true in the story?

Classifications

B2

What is the relationship between happiness and discontentment according to the author? Select at least three phrases or events in the story that illustrate the author's juxtaposition of these.

Details

B1

Cite examples of happiness versus discontentment in the story.

THE LOTTERY TICKET

Main Idea, Theme, or Concept

C3

Create a symbol that illustrates the main message of the story. Explain why you chose the symbol you did, using evidence from the text.

Inference

C2

How does the author's use of literary elements help us understand the characters' beliefs about wealth? Are the characters' beliefs about wealth realistic? Why or why not?

Literary Elements

C1

Explain how the author uses imagery and alliteration to emphasize certain events in the story. When is each used? Why?

THE LOTTERY TICKET

Using Emotion

E3

What is the importance of the lottery ticket on the couple's expectations? How does this compare with times you have had expectations that haven't come to fruition? Write the words "Lottery Ticket" vertically on a piece of paper and create an acrostic poem that highlights the emotional aspects of the ticket on the couple's lives.

Expressing Emotion

E2

Explain a time when an unexpected event changed your life. Was that event positive or negative? How did you react? Predictably? Unpredictably? What lesson did you learn? How does this compare with the lesson in the story?

Understanding Emotion

E1

Do you think the characters in the story expected their reaction to winning? Why or why not? Use examples from the text.

THE LOTTERY TICKET

Culminating Activity: Short Stories Section

Think about the short stories in this section that you have read. Select two stories that have similar themes, such as change, cause and effect, power, etc. What is the theme you chose? Use that theme and two short stories to complete the ladder on page 80.

SHORT STORIES

Generalizations

B3

Write an essay or create a detailed infographic that illustrates specific examples of how the theme you chose is evident in both stories. Be sure to justify your ideas by citing specific literary elements, quotes, plot features, or interactions between multiple story elements (i.e., characters and setting) and how these elements justify the theme you selected. Use the information from B1 and B2 to help you organize your essay or infographic.

Classifications

B2

Compare both lists and organize the lists into two or three categories about your theme.

Details

B1

What details or literary elements in each story are used to help convey the meaning of the theme you chose? Make a list for each story with specific examples from the text.

CHAPTER

2

Poetry

The following section of *Jacob's Ladder* focuses on selections of classical poetry, both British and American, with corresponding ladders that fit the selection chosen.

The poetry selections with their corresponding ladders are as follows:

Title	Ladder Skills
Weathers	A, D
Sonnet 73	A, C
The Clod and the Pebble	B, C
Hope Is the Thing With Feathers	D, E
Joy in the Woods	A, B, C
The Wild Swans at Coole	B, C, D
Not They Who Soar	B, C, D

Weathers

By Thomas Hardy

I

This is the weather the cuckoo likes,
And so do I;
When showers betumble the chestnut spikes,
And nestlings fly:
And the little brown nightingale bills his best,
And they sit outside at "The Travellers' Rest,"
And maids come forth sprig-muslin drest,
And citizens dream of the south and west,
And so do I.

II

This is the weather the shepherd shuns,
And so do I;
When beeches drip in brown and duns,
And thresh and ply;
And hill-hid tides throb, throe on throe,
And meadow rivulets overflow,
And drops on gate-bars hang in a row,
And rooks in families homeward go,
And so do I.

Consequences and Implications

A3

What are the implications of the repetitive words and phrases in each stanza on the reader (i.e., "and" and "and so do I")? Would the poem be as effective without these words and phrases? Why or why not?

Cause and Effect

A2

What are the effects of the two different seasons on the author? Use specific examples and phrases from the poem to explain.

Sequencing

A1

How does the sequence of each stanza help us understand what the author is saying about different seasons?

WEATHERS

Creative Synthesis

D3

Create your own poem that consists of two contrasting events. Include a transition statement to link them together.

Summarizing

D2

Compare and contrast the two stanzas of the poem. Explain how they fit together.

Paraphrasing

D1

Draw a picture of Stanza 1 and Stanza 2 based on the language from the poem. Be prepared to defend your illustrations.

WEATHERS

Sonnet 73

By William Shakespeare

That time of year thou mayst in me behold
When yellow leaves, or none, or few, do hang
Upon those boughs which shake against the cold,
Bare ruin'd choirs, where late the sweet birds sang.
In me thou seest the twilight of such day
As after sunset fadeth in the west,
Which by and by black night doth take away,
Death's second self, that seals up all in rest.
In me thou see'st the glowing of such fire
That on the ashes of his youth doth lie,
As the death-bed whereon it must expire
Consumed with that which it was nourish'd by.
This thou perceivest, which makes thy love more strong,
To love that well which thou must leave ere long.

Consequences and Implications

A3

What do the last two lines mean in relationship to the rest of the poem? Why doesn't Shakespeare discuss love until the end?

Cause and Effect

A2

According to the poem, what effect does nearing the end of life have on Shakespeare?

Sequencing

A1

How does Shakespeare describe the sequence of life toward death?

SONNET 73

Main Idea, Theme, or Concept

C3

Do you think this is a poem of reflection on the passing of time, self-pity about aging, life and death, or another concept? Create a concept map that connects phrases and identifies literary elements from the poem to support the concept you choose.

Inference

C2

What did Shakespeare mean by the phrase "As after sunset fadeth in the west, / Which by and by black night doth take away"?

Literary Elements

C1

Make a list of symbols and images in the poem and what they mean.

SONNET 73

The Clod and the Pebble
By William Blake

"Love seeketh not itself to please,
Nor for itself hath any care,
But for another gives its ease,
And builds a heaven in hell's despair."

So sung a little Clod of Clay,
Trodden with the cattle's feet,
But a Pebble of the brook
Warbled out these metres meet:

"Love seeketh only Self to please,
To bind another to its delight,
Joys in another's loss of ease,
And builds a hell in heaven's despite."

Generalizations

B3

What is the main message about love in the
poem? Write two generalizations.

Classifications

B2

How would you categorize the difference in the clod's
and pebble's views of love according to the poem?

Details

B1

What details in the poem suggest that the poem
is about different types of love?

THE CLOD AND THE PEBBLE

Main Idea, Theme, or Concept

C3

Write a poem in the style of Blake's poem that provides contrasting views about a feeling, emotion, or characteristic, such as trust, greed, anger, happiness, etc., and includes figurative language. Be prepared to share your poem and discuss how your poem is similar to Blake's style.

Inference

C2

Why might the poet use a clod of clay and a pebble for the different views of love? What makes each fitting for the type of love it represents?

Literary Elements

C1

Highlight the rhyming pattern in the poem. What do you know about the second stanza? Explain why Blake veers from an ABAB rhyming pattern in part of the second stanza only. Where does the change of view from one type of love to another occur? How does he let the readers know he is changing ideas?

Hope Is the Thing With Feathers

By Emily Dickinson

Hope is the thing with feathers
That perches in the soul,
And sings the tune—without the words,
And never stops at all,
And sweetest in the gale is heard;
And sore must be the storm
That could abash the little bird
That kept so many warm.
I've heard it in the chillest land,
And on the strangest sea;
Yet, never, in extremity,
It asked a crumb of me.

Creative Synthesis

D3

Create a poem to illustrate your feelings
about hope. Select a metaphor other than a bird
(i.e., Hope is _____). Compare your poem to Dickinson's.

Summarizing

D2

Summarize Dickinson's view of hope. Why might she
compare it to a bird versus another animal or object?

Paraphrasing

D1

In your own words, explain the meaning of
the last two lines of the poem.

HOPE IS THE THING WITH FEATHERS

Using Emotion

E3

If this poem were an illustration instead of a poem, what would it look like? Why?

Sketch an illustration that conveys the emotion of hope or another feeling you substitute based on Dickinson's poem. Be prepared to explain your images and colors used, as they convey emotion. Write a caption.

Expressing Emotion

E2

What other feelings besides hope might you add as essential ingredients for coping with life's demands?

Understanding Emotion

E1

How does Dickinson feel about hope as a support for the demands of life?

HOPE IS THE THING WITH FEATHERS

Joy in the Woods

By Claude McKay

There is joy in the woods just now,
The leaves are whispers of song,
And the birds make mirth on the bough
And music the whole day long,
And God! to dwell in the town
In these springlike summer days,
On my brow an unfading frown
And hate in my heart always—

A machine out of gear, aye, tired,
Yet forced to go on—for I'm hired.

Just forced to go on through fear,
For every day I must eat
And find ugly clothes to wear,
And bad shoes to hurt my feet
And a shelter for work-drugged sleep!
A mere drudge! but what can one do?
A man that's a man cannot weep!
Suicide? A quitter? Oh, no!

But a slave should never grow tired,
Whom the masters have kindly hired.

But oh! for the woods, the flowers
Of natural, sweet perfume,
The heartening, summer showers
And the smiling shrubs in bloom,
Dust-free, dew-tinted at morn,
The fresh and life-giving air,
The billowing waves of corn
And the birds' notes rich and clear:—

For a man-machine toil-tired
May crave beauty too—though he's hired.

Consequences and Implications

A3

What are implications of being bound versus free according to the author? Is his message still true today? Select a current event and compare the issues faced today with the concerns the author writes about in his poem.

Cause and Effect

A2

What is the relationship of the woods to the mental state of the narrator? What effect does the woods have on him? How does he contrast that with hired work? Create a T-chart to show the contrast of the woods to being hired. An example has been started for you.

Woods	Hired work
Joy in the woods just now	And God! to dwell in the town In these springlike summer days, On my brow an unfading frown And hate in my heart always—

Sequencing

A1

What are details from the poem that describe the woods? Draw a picture that depicts at least 4–5 of them and label the objects noted. Then highlight or underline the references to the woods listed throughout the poem. Why is the placement of when the author talks about the woods important?

Generalizations

B3

What generalizations might you make about the role of effective language in creating poetry? State two.

Classifications

B2

How would you categorize the effectiveness of the devices in the poem to create meaning? Why are these effective or ineffective?

Details

B1

McKay uses several poetic devices in the poem. A list has been started for you in the chart below. Provide examples of how these devices are used and what impact these devices have on the reader.

Device	Examples in Poem	Impact on Reader
Alliteration		
Repetition		
Rhyming Scheme		
Imagery		
Other devices		

C3

Main Idea, Theme, or Concept

Create a new title for the poem that includes your sense of what the poem means or the main message the author is trying to convey to society.

C2

Inference

What inferences do you draw from McKay's use of the hyphenated words, hyphens, and punctuated phrases with exclamation points? What images do these create? How do these help us understand the author's purpose and the meaning of the poem?

C1

Literary Elements

Do you think the narrator of the poem is the author or an imagined character? What evidence supports your ideas? In what time period was this poem set, based on the evidence included? How would you describe the narrator based on the evidence provided? Find out additional information about McKay's life, in addition to the evidence in the poem, to support your answer.

JOY IN THE WOODS

The Wild Swans at Coole

By William Butler Yeats

The trees are in their autumn beauty,
The woodland paths are dry,
Under the October twilight the water
Mirrors a still sky;
Upon the brimming water among the stones
Are nine-and-fifty swans.

The nineteenth autumn has come upon me
Since I first made my count;
I saw, before I had well finished,
All suddenly mount
And scatter wheeling in great broken rings
Upon their clamorous wings.

I have looked upon those brilliant creatures,
And now my heart is sore.
All's changed since I, hearing at twilight,
The first time on this shore,
The bell-beat of their wings above my head,
Trod with a lighter tread.

Unwearied still, lover by lover,
They paddle in the cold
Companionable streams or climb the air;
Their hearts have not grown old;
Passion or conquest, wander where they will,
Attend upon them still.

But now they drift on the still water,
Mysterious, beautiful;
Among what rushes will they build,
By what lake's edge or pool
Delight men's eyes when I awake some day
To find they have flown away?

Generalizations

B3

Write two true statements about the author's feelings about changes over time as conveyed in this poem.

Classifications

B2

How would you categorize the author's general mood when writing this poem? Why? Label each stanza with the mood of the author based on the words and descriptions.

Details

B1

This poem evokes many feelings. How does this poem make you feel? What details and phrases evoke specific feelings and why?

THE WILD SWANS AT COOLE

Main Idea, Theme, or Concept

C3

Many experts suggest that this poem is about the inevitability of aging and the life cycle. Do you agree or disagree? Why?

Inference

C2

How does the author's description of the swans relate to the human condition?

Literary Elements

C1

Yeats uses symbolism to express deeper meaning in the poem. Create a two-column chart that lists the symbols in Column 1 and what each symbolizes in Column 2. Be sure to include the symbols of autumn, swan, and twilight in addition to your own ideas.

Symbols	Meaning

Creative Synthesis

D3

Respond to the following question in a persuasive essay using information you learned in the previous two ladder rungs and your analysis of the poem to justify your thinking: Is "The Wild Swans at Coole" an autobiographical poem for Yeats?

Summarizing

D2

Organize the information you found into five summary statements about Yeats' life and writing.

Paraphrasing

D1

Research the author's life. Include the following information as part of your research: stage of life in which he was most successful as a poet; typical patterns and themes in his poetry; time period in which he wrote; general facts about his life (i.e., family, hardship, successes, interesting facts); stage of life when he wrote this poem; and the writing that came after it?

THE WILD SWANS AT COOLE

Not They Who Soar

By Paul Laurence Dunbar

Not they who soar, but they who plod
Their rugged way, unhelped, to God
Are heroes; they who higher fare,
And, flying, fan the upper air,
Miss all the toil that hugs the sod.
'Tis they whose backs have felt the rod,
Whose feet have pressed the path unshod,
May smile upon defeated care,
Not they who soar.

High up there are no thorns to prod,
Nor boulder lurking 'neath the clod
To turn the keenness of the share,
For flight is ever free and rare;
But heroes they the soil who've trod,
Not they who soar!

Generalizations

B3

What generalizations does Dunbar make
about slavery? Write at least two.

Classifications

B2

How does Dunbar categorize those who are
enslaved and those who are free?

Details

B1

List the ways in which Dunbar uses specific language to portray
the differences between those who are free versus those who
are slaves. What differences and similarities do you notice?

NOT THEY WHO SOAR

NOT THEY WHO SOAR

Main Idea, Theme, or Concept

C3

How does Dunbar portray freedom and slavery? Can one exist without the other? Create an image to convey your understanding of the relationship. Share with others in the class.

Inference

C2

What is meant by "they who higher fare, / And, flying, fan the upper air, / Miss all the toil that hugs the sod."?

Literary Elements

C1

Who are "they who soar"?

Creative Synthesis

D3

Create a new title that reflects Dunbar's intent for the poem.

Summarizing

D2

Find out more about Dunbar and the time period in which he wrote this poem. Summarize his life and the era in which he lived. How does his life story contribute to the overall meaning of the poem?

Paraphrasing

D1

Who are the heroes in the poem? How do you know?

NOT THEY WHO SOAR

Culminating Activity: Comparing "Wild Swans at Coole" and "Sonnet 73"

Revisit the poems "Wild Swans at Coole" and "Sonnet 73." Using these poems, complete the ladder on page 107.

Generalizations

B3

Write two generalizations that would be true of the message of each poem. Include at least three of the following concepts: change, time, life cycle, aging, loss of youth, regret.

Classifications

B2

How would you categorize the overall emphasis of each poem and the intended meaning? To what extent are the poems' messages the same or different? Compare and contrast each by creating a concept map for each poem.

Details

B1

What details are used in each poem to convey the authors' views on aging? Compare and contrast each poet's use of tone, mood, and metaphors to convey their message.

"WILD SWANS AT COOLE" AND "SONNET 73"

Culminating Activity: Comparing "Hope Is the Thing With Feathers" and "Not They Who Soar"

Revisit the poems "Hope Is the Thing With Feathers" and "Not They Who Soar." Using these poems, complete the ladder on page 109.

Creative Synthesis

D3

Create a dialogue (in written form or as a skit) between Dickinson and Dunbar about their views of the hardships of life and how to overcome them. Make sure each individual uses evidence from his or her writing in the responses as each conveys his or her views.

Summarizing

D2

How would each poet summarize his or her message for coping with hardships? How are their purposes similar and different?

Paraphrasing

D1

What details in each poem suggest that the author is writing about life's hardships?

"HOPE IS THE THING WITH FEATHERS" AND "NOT THEY WHO SOAR"

CHAPTER

3

Biographies

This chapter of *Jacob's Ladder* focuses on the use of biography as a specialized form of nonfiction in order to enhance students' understanding of their own career development, and to teach metacognitive skills in the process. The use of Ladders E and F is evident in this section. Once students have completed the four biographies, additional analysis activities are included that encourage comparative analyses across the biographies.

The list of biographies with their ladders is found below:

Title	Ladder Skills
Erwin Schrödinger, physicist	A, B
Amartya Sen, economist	A, B
Harriet Tubman, social reformer	C, E
Marie Curie, scientist	A, C
Margaret Mead, anthropologist	B, F
Lin-Manuel Miranda, composer, playwright, and lyricist	B, D

Erwin Schrödinger
Physicist

Considered to be one of the most important contributors to the field of theoretical physics, Erwin Schrödinger is celebrated today as a father of quantum mechanics, and the importance of his work is equated with that of Isaac Newton. Although he lived during the tumultuous years of World War I and World War II, moving frequently from country to country, he managed to make conceptual breakthroughs in quantum theory and shared the Nobel Prize in 1933.

Erwin was born in 1887 in Vienna to Rudolf Schrödinger and Georgine Emilia Brenda. His parents were well educated, and his father studied chemistry, Italian painting, and botany. Young Erwin was bilingual, speaking German and English, and was homeschooled until he was 11. In 1898, he entered a renowned secondary school in Vienna, where he studied until 1906. Although he loved science, he was also fond of language arts and poetry. This multidisciplinary appreciation, likely inspired by his father's many interests, continued to guide him throughout his schooling.

In 1906, he entered the University of Vienna, where he studied physics and laid the groundwork for his later work in quantum mechanics. He received his doctorate in 1910 and continued to work in academia for several years until World War I broke out. In 1914, Erwin served as an artillery officer on the Italian front. His mind was never far from his work, however, and he managed to publish from his post. Unfortunately, Erwin's mentor, physicist Friedrich Hasenöhrl, was killed during the war. Erwin would later dedicate an award to his late professor.

After the war, Erwin married and worked at several universities, never staying in one place for long, until he settled at the University of Zurich for 6 years. He enjoyed his colleagues and friendships at Zurich, writing papers on theoretical physics, thermodynamics, and even studies of color. It was during this time that he started his well-known work with wave mechanics, originally inspired by a footnote in a paper by Albert Einstein. Erwin's famous equation sought to explain the movement of an electron within an atom as a wave, which was revolutionary in 1926. Many scientists enjoyed his wave theory because it was easier to visualize than the strictly mathematical conception that had preceded it.

In 1927, bolstered by his success, Erwin accepted a position at the University of Berlin. His time in Berlin was productive for teaching and learning, but the rise of the Nazi party there made Erwin deeply uncomfortable. He denounced the anti-Semitic viewpoints of the rising party as many of his colleagues were forced to leave their jobs or flee the country. In 1933, when Hitler became chancellor, Erwin managed to leave Germany with his wife. Unfortunately, the Nazi party considered his leaving an unfriendly act.

At Oxford University, Erwin learned that he, along with fellow physicist Paul Dirac, had won the Nobel Prize in Physics. However, tensions arose at Oxford because of Erwin's unconventional lifestyle. Although he was married to Annemarie Bertel, he had several affairs throughout their marriage, and even had children with other women. Oxford did not approve of the relationships, and Erwin eventually moved on because of the escalating tension.

Soon after he left Oxford, Erwin made history again. In an informal correspondence with Albert Einstein, Erwin proposed a thought experiment, now referred to as Schrödinger's Cat. Erwin proposed the paradox to help illustrate a problem he noticed in a certain interpretation of quantum mechanics. In this paradox, a cat sits inside a sealed box with a certain amount of poison that might or might not be fatal. According to the logic of the interpretation, until a scientist opens the box to measure the result, the cat is both alive and dead. Of course, Erwin explained, this cannot be the case, so there must be some flaw in the underlying theory. Erwin's conception of the paradox influenced thinkers for the next century and caused much debate in the scientific community, inspiring others to write their own challenging variations of the experiment.

In 1936, Erwin attempted to return to Austria, but the country had been occupied by Germany by that time, and he encountered trouble there. His denouncement of Nazism and abrupt departure from Berlin years earlier had not been forgiven. Under mounting pressure, he attempted to recant his anti-Nazi sentiments (an act he would deeply regret later), but it was too late to find acceptance in Austria. Instead, he and his family escaped to Italy.

Finally, after more travel, Erwin settled in Dublin as the Director of the School of Theoretical Physics at the Institute for Advanced Studies. For the next 17 years, he worked and lived in Dublin, delivering many well-attended lectures. In 1944, he published a book, *What Is Life?*, in which he proposed that the genetic code for life might be housed in a complex molecule. His work was derived not only from scientific principles, but also by his philosophical beliefs. The publication of *What Is Life?* motivated Nobel Prize-winner Francis Crick, who would later name the book as the inspiration for his discovery of the double helix structure for DNA.

During his years in Dublin, Erwin continued to publish. Many of his papers at that time explored the possibility of a unified field theory, one that would unify Einstein's theories of relativity and electromagnetism. He shared these theories with Albert Einstein, and the two corresponded through letters until the mid-1940s.

As he grew older, Erwin turned to his old passions, Greek history and philosophy. Work in this area of interest yielded a series of lectures, which were later transcribed into books entitled *Nature and the Greeks* and *Science and Humanism*. The lectures and the books were hailed as succinct and brilliant successes.

In 1955, Erwin retired, and a year later he left Dublin for his native Vienna. One year later, he was asked to give a lecture on nuclear energy at the World Energy Conference; however, he refused on the grounds that he did not believe nuclear energy was possible. Instead, he gave a lecture on the philosophy of science. In later years, his interest in the unified field theory and general relativity continued, although he caused some controversy when he abandoned the traditional view of wave-particle duality, which relies on statistical approximations, in favor of a wave-only approach.

Erwin died of tuberculosis in Vienna in 1961. He left behind many writings and discoveries that helped advance the field of quantum physics. Although he led an unconventional lifestyle and often courted unnecessary controversy, he remains an excellent example of dedication to one's work. Even with the chaos and disruption of the World Wars, he managed to commit himself to his work and contribute to the field in groundbreaking ways.

References

Mastin, L. (2009). *Erwin Schrödinger (1887–1961)*. Retrieved from http://www.physicsoftheuniverse.com/scientists_schrodinger.html

The Nobel Foundation. (1965). Erwin Schrödinger—biographical. In *The Nobel Lectures, Physics 1922–1941*. Amsterdam, The Netherlands: Elsevier. Retrieved from http://www.nobelprize.org/nobel_prizes/physics/laureates/1933/schrodinger-bio.html

WBGH. (1998). *Erwin Schrödinger: 1887–1961*. Retrieved from http://www.pbs.org/wgbh/aso/databank/entries/bpschr.html

Consequences and Implications

A3

What would you say is the importance of collaboration and publication in a scientific field, based on Erwin Schrödinger's life?

Cause and Effect

A2

How did other scientists' discoveries and publications affect Erwin Schrödinger's own success?

Sequencing

A1

In chronological order, list the colleagues who interacted with Erwin Schrödinger. Why do you think these individuals were included in his biography?

ERWIN SCHRÖDINGER

Generalizations

B3

Write a generalization, based on Erwin Schrödinger's life,
that explains what it takes to be an eminent scientist.
(Use the words from your categories to help you.)

Classifications

B2

Organize his personal characteristics into at least three
different categories. What categories did you choose? Why?

Details

B1

What personal characteristics made Erwin Schrödinger
a successful scientist? Highlight and label examples
of these characteristics in the biography.

ERWIN SCHRÖDINGER

Amartya Sen
Economist

Amartya Sen is an eminent, Nobel Prize-winning economist and humanitarian renowned for his work in welfare economics. His theories have alerted modern economists to the injustice and inequalities experienced by the poverty-stricken, minorities, and women. He is often called "the Mother Teresa of economics."

Amartya was born into a family of academics on November 3, 1933. His birthplace was the college campus of Visva-Bharati in Santiniketan, West Bengal, India. The coeducational college, which was also a secondary school, was founded by Nobel Prize-winner and friend of the Sen family, Rabindranath Tagore. It was Tagore who gave Amartya his first name, which means "immortality" in Sanskrit. Amartya's grandfather, Kshitimohan Sen, taught Sanskrit and ancient Indian literature at the college, which was known for its commitment to progressive education. Amartya's father, Ashutosh Sen, was a professor of chemistry at Dhaka University, located in what is now Bangladesh. His mother, Amita Sen, edited a literary magazine in Bengal.

As a young boy, Amartya's parents moved from Dhaka to Bengal, where he attended classes at the Visva-Bharati school. There, he was encouraged to pursue a love of learning and curiosity rather than good grades; in fact, academic competition was frowned upon by the teachers. Even though his school supported acceptance of many diverse cultures, citizens in his community shunned their shared Indian identities in favor of strict identification with their different religious communities. Amartya witnessed the violent consequences of this shift in identities when, as a teenager, he saw a Muslim day laborer stagger onto the family's property, bleeding profusely from multiple stab wounds. As Amartya's father rushed the man, Kader Mia, to the hospital, he explained that he had chosen, against his wife's advice, to accept work in a Hindu neighborhood because his family desperately needed the money. Upon learning that he was Muslim, a group of Hindus stabbed him in the street. The bleeding man died later at the hospital, and Amartya was haunted by the poor man's story for the rest of his life. He concluded that poor economic conditions and social intolerance had left this man, and many more like him, vulnerable to injustice and violence. It was during this time that Amartya also saw the ruination caused by the 1943 famine in Bengal, which would claim millions of lives. The fact that Amartya's upper-middle-class family was unaffected, and only the poorest laborers went without food, would later inspire Amartya's economic theories.

Upon graduating from Visva-Bharati, Amartya moved to impoverished Calcutta, where he attended Presidency College and worked toward his bachelor's degree. He majored in economics, minored in mathematics, and enjoyed the heated political debates he met with as an undergraduate. He embraced political tolerance and values that were many times belittled by his left-leaning friends. It was a friend who first introduced Amartya to the work of economist Kenneth Arrow, whose book *Social Choice and Individual Values*, published in 1951, proposed what is now known as Arrow's impossibility theorem, the idea that all majority rules, including the status quo, cannot yield truly democratic outcomes. His book focused mainly on voting choice. This landmark book was the catalyst for Amartya's subsequent fascination with social choice theory, and Arrow's work would be the launching pad for Amartya's later work.

In 1952, Amartya was diagnosed with mouth cancer and underwent a harsh course of radiation. He recovered, and in 1953, he graduated from Calcutta University and left for Trinity College at Cambridge University in England. At the time, the economists at Cambridge were debating two different economic theories. Amartya identified with neither side, making him somewhat isolated in his interests. He was sheltered from the heat of this debate at Trinity College, where he studied under economists Maurice Dobb, Dennis Robertson, and Piero Sraffa, all of whom held different economic views but, nevertheless, got along together. He earned his degree in 1955 and promptly began work in his doctoral program at Cambridge.

As a doctoral student, Amartya took a 2-year leave to travel to Calcutta, where he was supervised in his doctoral thesis by the great A. K. Dasgupta, an economic methodologist who was instrumental as Amartya's mentor. Amartya was offered the position of Professor of Economics at Jadavpur University. He accepted at the young age of 23. Upon finishing his thesis, he submitted it to be considered for the Prize Fellowship at Trinity College. He won the award, which allowed him to study anything he chose for 4 years. After receiving his doctorate in 1959, Amartya spent the next 4 years studying philosophy at Cambridge. Amartya's interest in philosophy complemented his interest in welfare economics, and he later wrote several papers in philosophy.

In 1960, Amartya married his first wife, Nabaneeta Dev, whom he'd met while studying in India. They later had two daughters together, Nandana and Artara. The next year, Amartya escaped the still-broiling economic debates at Cambridge, and traveled to MIT and Stanford in the United States, where he was a visiting professor. Then, in 1963, he returned to India, where he taught economics at the University of Delhi.

Later, Amartya left India to accept a position at the prestigious London School of Economics, where he taught for 7 years.

In 1970, he published his remarkable work, *Collective Choice and Social Welfare*, which he had begun writing while still living in India. He was greatly aided in his endeavor by economists Kenneth Arrow and John Rawls, with whom he briefly taught a joint course at Harvard University. The book advanced the perspectives of welfare economics—that although governments should consider the best interest of the people, they should not concern themselves with defining perfect solutions to public welfare problems.

Within a year, Amartya and his family relocated to England, where Amartya was offered a faculty position at the prestigious London School of Economics. Although he was excited at the fresh intellectual opportunities the university offered, he suffered two major setbacks in his first years in England. First, his wife divorced him and returned to India. Second, Amartya suddenly began experiencing alarming symptoms that suggested his mouth cancer had returned. Alarmed, Amartya underwent exploratory surgery, during which doctors discovered that he suffered not from cancer, but from bone necrosis, due to the harmful course of radiation he'd received as an undergraduate in India. Amartya recovered after surgery, and went on to teach at the London School of Economics for the next 6 years. He met his second wife, Eva Colorni, who was an Italian economist. They later had two children. Eva encouraged Amartya to consider practical work, extending the social choice theory to more applied problems. In this way, she offered great support to Amartya, who felt she was a major influence on his work.

From 1977 to 1987, Amartya served in two faculty positions at Oxford University, and in 1981, he published his famous book entitled *Poverty and Famines: An Essay on Entitlement and Deprivation*. In this book, Amartya examined famines that had occurred in Africa, China, and India, noting that starvation was not determined by an inadequate distribution of food, but rather by social factors (e.g., low wages, increased food costs, unemployment). The book also recalled Amartya's experiences in the Bengal famine of 1943. He noted that food supplies were actually more plentiful the year of the famine than they had been in previous nonfamine years. However, landless laborers were not paid enough to afford inflated food prices, which skyrocketed in response to British military and war costs. Thus, the most impoverished communities were those who starved, while middle-class and upper class families were left unscathed.

The early 1980s were a productive time for Amartya, who, with Eva's encouragement, published three more books, including one on the role played by gender inequalities in starvation, *Commodities and Capabilities*. Although Amartya received acclaim for these works, he also experienced tragedy. His wife Eva died suddenly in the early 1980s. Wanting a change of scene, Amartya left England to accept a faculty position at Harvard University. He taught there from 1988 to 1998, during which time he published the essay "Gender and Cooperative Conflicts," an empirical review of statistics concerning gender differences combined with comparative data Amartya collected in the field. This was followed by another book, *Inequality Reexamined*, which further explored his capability approach to welfare economics. In 1998, Amartya's contributions to the field of economics were awarded the highest honor, the Nobel Prize in Economic Science. In keeping with his devotion to equality and humanitarian aid, Amartya used his prize money to establish the Pratichi Trust, which helps fund programs and works that fight against famine.

From 1998 to 2003, Amartya was Master of Trinity College, the first person of Indian descent to fill this position. Following this post, he returned to Harvard University, where he currently sits as the Thomas W. Lamont University Professor of Economics. In addition to his Nobel Prize, Amartya was also awarded the Bharat Ratna (Jewel of India), which is the highest honor awarded to a civilian for public service by the President of India. He is now remarried to economic historian Emma Georgina Rothschild, with whom he makes an annual sojourn to India. Beloved in his native country and around the world, Amartya is widely considered to be the conscience of economics. He has dedicated his career to illuminating the plights of the impoverished and neglected populations across the globe, giving voice to millions whose suffering has been ignored by governments, academia, and their fellow countrymen.

References

Encyclopaedia Brittanica. (2016). *Amartya Sen: Indian Economist*. Retrieved from https://www.britannica.com/biography/Amartya-Sen

Encyclopedia.com. (2004). *Sen, Amartya Kumar*. Retrieved from http://www.encyclopedia.com/people/history/historians-ancient-biographies/amartya-sen

Indobase. (1993). *Indians abroad: Amartya Sen*. Retrieved from http://www.indobase.com/indians-abroad/amartya-sen.html

The Nobel Foundation. (1998). *Amartya Sen—Biographical*. Retrieved from http://www.nobelprize.org/nobel_prizes/economic-sciences/laureates/1998/sen-bio.html

Steele, J. (2001). Food for thought. *The Guardian*. Retrieved from https://www.theguardian.com/books/2001/mar/31/society.politics

Consequences and Implications

A3

What implications did Amartya Sen's early experiences and dedication to injustice have on the field of economics?

Cause and Effect

A2

What effect did Amartya Sen's childhood experiences and socioeconomic status have on his future career path?

Sequencing

A1

Sequence the major positive and negative events leading up to Amartya Sen's success. Which events and life circumstances were most important to his future? Why?

AMARTYA SEN

Generalizations

B3

Create an outline for a public service announcement that educates others about an injustice based on an issue or event that impacted you; include at least one generalization about the injustice and refer to Amartya Sen's work and others in your ad.

Classifications

B2

Think of a time when you were deeply moved by a person's story or event. What did you do? How did you react? How did you (or could you have) use your gifts and resources for the betterment of the situation or person? Write a wish list of how you would like to make a difference in the world and categorize it by the types of actions you might take.

Details

B1

How did Amartya Sen use his feelings about poverty for good? State the details in his life that contributed to this positive motive.

AMARTYA SEN

Harriet Tubman
Social Reformer

Harriet Tubman was born Araminta Ross to slaves Harriet and Ben Ross in Maryland sometime around 1820. No reliable records were kept of slave births, so she may actually have been born as late as 1825. Her owner, Edward Brodess, ran a farm and raised slaves to sell or rent out to nearby plantations for labor. Araminta was first put to work when she was only 6 or 7 years old, taking care of an infant in a home where she was beaten when the baby cried. She was permanently scarred from whippings she received in her childhood, but she was rebellious and clever even at a young age. She began wearing several layers of clothing to protect herself from the whip.

In her early teens, Araminta began working in the fields. It was around this time that she began calling herself Harriet, after her mother. One day, while running an errand for her master, she saw a slave attempting to run away. The overseer ordered Harriet to restrain the slave, but she refused, blocking the doorway so the slave could run away. The outraged overseer hurled a 2-pound lead weight that struck Harriet in the head. She was knocked unconscious and remained in a coma for some time. It took her several months to recover, and as soon as she could stand, she was sent back out for hard labor. She sustained permanent damage from this blow, and for the rest of her life she suffered from seizures, headaches, and sudden bouts of unconsciousness.

Sometime around 1844, Harriet married a free Black man named John Tubman. However, she was still a slave, so even though she slept at John's house every night, she still had to get up every day and suffer the indignities of slavery. When Brodess died in 1849, though, Harriet's family was at risk of being torn apart forever in separate sales to various landowners. Harriet had heard rumors about the Underground Railroad, a secret connection between homes, or "stations," of White and Black abolitionists on the way to Canada and free states in the North. She decided that this was her chance to escape. A White woman who lived nearby gave her a name and directions to the first station she would stop at, and Harriet and two of her brothers ran away on foot in the middle of the night. Her brothers were afraid of the consequences should they be caught, so they turned back. Harriet went on alone,

HARRIET TUBMAN.

traveling at night, using the North Star as her guide along with help from the Underground Railroad "conductors" she encountered on her path to freedom.

She made it to Philadelphia, PA, and began cooking, cleaning, and saving up to go back and rescue her family. In Philadelphia, she met other abolitionists and determined that her life's calling was to conduct as many slaves to freedom as she possibly could. In 1850, she returned to Maryland and escorted her sister to freedom in Canada. Over the next 7 years, Harriet returned three times to rescue her brothers and parents, relocating all of them to her base of operations in Canada. She tried to bring her husband along with her, but in the time she had been gone, he found another wife. Tubman did not seem to be very affected by this. She continued making trips—19 in all—before the Civil War began. During this time, she acquired several nicknames: "Moses" because she led around 300 people out of slavery and "General Tubman" because of her no-nonsense attitude. Harriet was very serious about getting every one of her "passengers" to safety. To this end, she carried a gun and threatened to shoot anyone who got scared and turned back. She proudly told Frederick Douglass that she "never lost a single passenger," in spite of her uncontrollable sleeping spells. By the time the Civil War began, the reward for Harriet Tubman's capture was $40,000, which today would be equivalent to more than one million dollars. She was well known in the North and the South but still managed to evade capture with help from some famous abolitionist friends, including New York Senator and Abraham Lincoln's future Secretary of State William H. Seward and his wife. In fact, she stayed in the Sewards' house for a period of time, and in 1859 they sold it to her for a very low price. She moved her family from Canada into the house in Auburn, NY.

Controversial abolitionist John Brown also became a friend to Harriet, and she reportedly helped him plan the raid on Harpers Ferry, VA, in 1859. When the Civil War broke out in 1860, she worked for the Union Army in a variety of ways. She was a cook, nurse, and even a spy, scouting Confederate territories and reporting back to the Union army. In fact, she even commanded a military raid—the first woman to do so—when she led Colonel Montgomery and the men of the 2nd South Carolina regiment in the decimation of Confederate supply depots and the freeing of more than 700 slaves. Despite her dedication and service, Tubman was not awarded a veteran's pension and therefore struggled financially for the rest of her life.

After the war, she went back to Auburn, NY, and continued her humanitarian work. She took up the suffragist cause, fighting for women's right to vote, and transformed her home into a Home for Aged and Indigent Colored People in 1868. In 1867, John Tubman, no longer connected to

Harriet, died. Two years later, Harriet married Nelson Davis, a fellow veteran of the Civil War. That same year, she and Sarah Bradford cowrote her biography, which somewhat eased her money troubles. When her second husband died in 1888, she finally received money from the government in the form of a widow's pension. She was invited to speak publicly and worked closely with the African Methodist Episcopal Zion Church, which would take over running the home she founded when Harriet herself was admitted in 1911. After her death in 1913, she was laid to rest in Fort Hill Cemetery with full military honors.

References

Biography.com. (2017). *Harriet Tubman*. Retrieved from https://www.biography.com/people/harriet-tubman-9511430

Harriet Tubman Historical Society. (2017). *Harriet Tubman*. Retrieved from http://www.harriet-tubman.org

History.com. (2009). *Harriet Tubman*. Retrieved from http://www.history.com/topics/black-history/harriet-tubman

New York History Net. (n.d.) *The life of Harriet Tubman*. Retrieved from http://www.nyhistory.com/harriettubman/life.htm

PBS Black Culture Connection. (2017). *Explore: Harriet Tubman*. Retrieved from http://www.pbs.org/black-culture/explore/harriet-tubman/#.WXoCdojyuUk

Wikipedia. (2017). *Harriet Tubman*. Retrieved from https://en.wikipedia.org/wiki/Harriet_Tubman

Main Idea, Theme, or Concept

C3

Overcoming extreme adversity and external limitations was a huge part of Harriet Tubman's life and ultimate work in freeing slaves. Create a symbol or metaphor for Harriet Tubman's life work that illustrates how passion, negative life experiences, and working for a cause can be beneficial in motivating one to succeed.

Inference

C2

Assess the characteristics Harriet Tubman displayed in her work as an abolitionist. Which of these do you identify with and why? How might such characteristics help you in your planning to become a professional in a given field?

Literary Elements

C1

How did Harriet Tubman decide to become a social reformer? What factors influenced her? What factors have influenced you so far in your thinking about your life work?

HARRIET TUBMAN

Using Emotion

E3

How did Harriet Tubman use her early experiences to transform herself in adulthood? What negative experiences have you had in your life that can be used for good in the future? Describe and reflect on how to use these experiences to your advantage.

Expressing Emotion

E2

Write a poem or draw a picture to depict your feelings about Harriet Tubman and her life.

Understanding Emotion

E1

What emotions might Harriet Tubman have had when she was shepherding slaves into freedom? How did others feel about her? Give examples from her biography.

HARRIET TUBMAN

Marie Curie
Scientist

When Maria Sklodowska was born in 1867, Warsaw, Poland was hardly recognizable. At the time, Poland was under occupation by Austria, Russia, and Prussia, and Warsaw was under Russian control. Oppressive Russian laws prohibited proper math and science classes from being taught at the boarding schools where Maria's parents worked. Her father was a physicist, however, and both parents ensured that Maria and her brother and sisters received a well-rounded education. Maria's mother died of tuberculosis when Maria was only 11 years old, and although she was devastated, she continued to work hard with her tutors.

Maria was always at the top of her class even though she was in classes with older girls. She and her sister Bronislawa (Bronya) joined an illegal night school dubbed the "Floating University," because the location had to change constantly to avoid detection by the Russians. At the Floating University, they studied many subjects, always with a political mind toward bringing about the eventual independence of the Polish nation. Eventually, the sisters realized they needed a more formal education and made a pact: Maria would work to support Bronya's medical education in Paris, and when Bronya had amassed enough funds, she would bring Maria to Paris and support her education in turn.

With Bronya away in Paris, 16-year-old Maria began giving private tutoring lessons in Warsaw. She worked for 2 years but did not make enough money to support both Bronya's and her own dreams, so she moved to a small factory village and worked for the factory's owner as governess to his children. After 3 years at this job, and with a little help from her father, Maria was finally able to move to Paris in 1891 to begin studying at Paris-Sorbonne University. It was here that she changed her name to the French spelling, Marie.

Marie got her degree in physics in 2 years, followed by a degree in math a year later, as well as a master's degree in physics. In 1894, she was working on her master's degree in mathematics in addition to a study of magnetism commissioned by the Society for the Encouragement of National Industry, and she needed laboratory facilities in which to work on it. She was introduced to Pierre Curie, who ran a lab in Paris at the School of Industrial Physics and Chemistry. Curie was already involved in studying magnetism, so it was a perfect match in more ways than one. Within the year, Marie and Pierre were married and hardly ever left their lab except to go bicycling across the French countryside.

Marie became a French citizen, but Poland was always on her mind. She applied for admittance to Krakow University but was denied—women were not yet permitted to attend. However, her fondness for Poland was not deterred. She hired Polish governesses to tutor both of her daughters in the Polish language. In 1898, when Pierre and Marie discovered a new element, they named it polonium.

In 1896, another French scientist named Henri Becquerel discovered that rays of energy similar to X-rays emitted from uranium without any outside source interacting with it. The Curies continued research on the phenomenon and called this inherent radiation "radioactivity." Marie figured out how to prove the existence of this strange energy by using a device, called the electrometer, previously invented by Pierre and his brother. By sampling the air around the uranium, she determined that the uranium was causing the air to conduct electrical currents. The Curies and Becquerel shared the 1903 Nobel Prize in Physics for these discoveries, but it was Marie who came up with the theory of radioactivity as well as the manner for measuring it.

Around the same time, the Curies had discovered yet another new radioactive element that they named radium. However, radium could only be found in scant traces; it took one ton of ore to isolate one tenth of a gram of radium. Marie and Pierre worked tirelessly to obtain pure radium metal even after Marie came up with a more efficient way of isolating the element. Many scientists, once they create such a process, immediately patent it so that they alone can freely use it. However, Marie saw the great possibilities for radium and decided not to patent it, thus granting the global scientific community free reign over radium research. In 1911, she won the Nobel Prize in Chemistry for her work with radium and the isolation process.

Tragedy struck the pair when Pierre was hit by a horse-drawn wagon while crossing the street and died. Grief-stricken but determined to continue their work, Marie began teaching his classes and eventually took his post as professor of general physics, having earned her doctoral degree in 1903. She was the first female professor at the Sorbonne. Marie brilliantly saw the potential for radium in the medical field, as radioactivity could be used for imaging machines. During World War I, she and her daughter outfitted vehicles and trained 150 nurses with X-ray technology so that medics could find bullets and shrapnel in wounded soldiers and perform emergency surgery on the battlefield without moving the patients.

Marie Curie founded and directed the Radium Institute in Paris, which was renamed the Curie Institute after her death. She also founded the Radium Institute in Warsaw, which Bronya (by then a doctor) directed; it was also renamed for her posthumously. She received two Nobel Prizes and various other scientific accolades. Her daughter, Irène Joliot-Curie, went on to win the Nobel Prize in Chemistry in 1935. Marie Curie's influence on modern physics and medicine is truly remarkable. Unfortunately, her dedication and devotion to her work led to her demise. She died of leukemia in 1934—attributed to her decades-long exposure to radioactive elements.

References

American Physical Society. (2017). *December 1898: The Curies discover radium*. Retrieved from https://www.aps.org/publications/apsnews/200412/history.cfm

Gwiazdowska, B., & Bulski, W. (1998). *Marie Curie: The founder of the Radium Institute in Warsaw*. Retrieved from http://www.thegreenjournal.com/article/S0167-8140(98)00139-X/pdf

Mahar, P. (2017). *The petite Curies of World War One*. Retrieved from https://argunners.com/marie-curie-world-war-one

Margerison, C. (2011). *Meet Marie Curie, An eStory: Inspirational stories*. Retrieved from https://books.google.com/books?id=dX6VFqlxkSsC&pg=PT14&lpg=PT14&dq=how+did+marie+curie+became+a+french+citizen&source=bl&ots=guIuWYLvfX&sig=ASz8GcLcRBjTEvtiL8fCj5F4wtk&hl=en&sa=X&ved=0ahUKEwjQ1OWejazVAhWFQSYKHbSDDZ0Q6AEIXjAI#v=onepage&q=how%20did%20marie%20curie%20became%20a%20french%20citizen&f=false

Oudar, N. (2017). *Our history*. Retrieved from https://institut-curie.org/page/our-history

Pasachoff, N. (2000). *Marie Curie and the science of radioactivity*. Retrieved from https://history.aip.org/exhibits/curie/polgirl1.htm

Podogrocka, E. (n.d.). *Bronislawa Dluska*. Retrieved from http://www.unless-women.eu/biography-details/items/dluska.html

Schools Wikipedia Selection. (2008/2009). *Marie Curie*. Retrieved from https://www.cs.mcgill.ca/~rwest/link-suggestion/wpcd_2008-09_augmented/wp/m/Marie_Curie.htm

Truman, C. (2017). *Marie Curie*. Retrieved from http://www.historylearningsite.co.uk/a-history-of-medicine/marie-curie

Consequences and Implications

A3

What were the implications of gender on
Marie Curie's accomplishments?

Cause and Effect

A2

How did the discovery of radium affect Marie Curie's later discoveries?

MARIE CURIE

Sequencing

A1

It is often said that one success leads to another. How is this illustrated
in the life of Marie Curie? Sequence the series of positive events.

Main Idea, Theme, or Concept

C3

If you were to write an epitaph for Marie Curie to be placed on her tombstone, what would it be? Why?

Inference

MARIE CURIE

C2

How did Marie Curie's gender and early life in Poland affect her career? What advice would you give to someone who is trying to break into a field that is dominated by a group that is different from that person? How does understanding Marie Curie's life help you provide this advice?

Literary Elements

C1

What were Marie Curie's strongest characteristics? How did these traits help her to be a successful scientist?

Margaret Mead
Anthropologist

One of the most widely read anthropologists and greatest minds of the 20th century, Margaret Mead was the first child born to Edward and Emily Fogg Mead in December 1901. They lived in Philadelphia, PA, and soon grew to be a family of six. Hers was a family that valued education, as her father was a professor of finance at the University of Pennsylvania, her mother was a respected sociologist and ethnologist, and her grandmother was a teacher who provided much of Margaret's schooling at home. Emily Mead liberally encouraged her children to pursue their passions and modeled acceptance of individuality. This would heavily influence Margaret's career later in life.

Margaret was initially interested in the humanities: poetry, theater, writing, and psychology. She spent one year of her undergraduate career at DePauw University but transferred to Barnard College in New York, where she got her degree in sociology in 1923. During her senior year, she took an anthropology course taught by Franz Boas, assisted by Ruth Benedict, and discovered her true passion. Ruth became her best friend and remained so throughout her life. Margaret started studying at Columbia University, where she got her master's degree in anthropology in 1925. After graduating, she traveled to Samoa, a Pacific island, to begin her field research.

Three years later, Mead published her first book, *Coming of Age in Samoa*. Her research focused on adolescence, a tumultuous time in the life of the American teenager. To her surprise, she found that the transition from girl to woman was free of psychological distress in Samoa. It was there that she began to conceive of the ideas that would drive much of her later research on the effects of socialization and cultural surroundings compared to biological influences on personality development.

After returning from Samoa, Margaret took the position of assistant curator at the American Museum of Natural History in New York in 1926. Although her professional relationship with the museum would grow over the next 40 years, she continued her research in the field. She conducted research with her second husband in New Guinea, studying adolescence in the Manus culture. She published *Growing Up in New Guinea* in 1930 and went right back into the field, studying three different cultures on mainland New Guinea. It was here that she discovered three vastly different sets of gender roles within a small geographical range. *Sex and Temperament in Three Primitive Societies* described the differences between the cultures and compared them to Western conventions. In one culture, the men and women were treated equally and shared equally the burdens of sustaining the family and raising the children. In another, the men and women were aggressive, hostile, and often left the children to tend to themselves. Finally, in the Tchambuli culture, she found a society of dominant women alongside men who looked after the home in what Westerners would call the "housewife" role.

All of these experiences led Margaret to believe that parents' and the culture's expectations shape the behavior of children much more so than biology. She disagreed with the notion that qualities of masculinity or femininity were inherent or genetic. She passionately defended her beliefs in several best-selling books and regular magazine columns. Because she was able to communicate clearly to the public at large, Margaret exposed many Americans to anthropology for the first time. She soon became a hotly debated household name. She welcomed criticism and dissent; she was just pleased that average Americans were discussing cultural anthropology. In 1936, she married her third and final husband, Gregory Bateson. He, like her previous two husbands, was also an anthropologist, and together they traveled and studied in Bali. At this time, film was not being widely used as a research tool, and Margaret was one of the first to document her subjects in photographs.

One of Margaret Mead's greatest contributions to the world was her adherence to a holistic approach to all aspects of life. She had a gift for incorporating every field and illuminating the connections between politics, history, anthropology, psychology, education, science, and so on. Above all, she emphasized the benefits of learning about other cultures in order to think more critically about one's own culture. During World War II, she and Ruth Benedict helped public policymakers address the issues of encountering many different cultures and soon formed the Institute for Intercultural Studies.

Margaret was crushed when Gregory left her in 1950, but she was likely comforted by her daughter, Mary Catherine Bateson. Mary Catherine also become a well-regarded anthropologist. In 1953, Margaret returned to the Manus culture in Samoa, 25 years after she had studied their young girls' adolescence. She understood the importance of longitudinal studies and encouraged anthropologists, historians, politicians, and the general public to consider changes over biological time rather than calendar years. "Biological time" refers to time as generations—about 25 years per generation. She urged people to be patient when waiting for political or cultural changes, warning against high hopes and promises of quick fixes.

Margaret Mead was truly one-of-a-kind. *TIME* magazine called her "Mother of the World," and by the time she passed away, people had begun referring to her as the grandmother of the world. She was a lecturer, professor at several universities, founder of numerous anthropology departments, and president of quite a few anthropological and scientific societies. She lived a life fuller than most people's and died in 1978 of cancer. Margaret was posthumously awarded the Presidential Medal of Freedom. She was an inspiration to many for her contributions and words of wisdom, and notably said, "Never doubt that a small group of thoughtful, committed citizens can change the world. Indeed, it is the only thing that ever has."

References

Biography.com. (2014). *Margaret Mead*. Retrieved from https://www.biography.com/people/margaret-mead-9404056

Dillon, W. (2001). *Margaret Mead (1901–1978)*. Retrieved from http://www.ibe.unesco.org/sites/default/files/meade.pdf

Encyclopedia of World Biography. (2017). *Margaret Mead biography*. Retrieved from http://www.notablebiographies.com/Ma-Mo/Mead-Margaret.html

Flaherty, T. (n.d.) *Margaret Mead, 1901–1978*. Retrieved from http://faculty.webster.edu/woolflm/margaretmead.html

Geertz, C. (1989). *Margaret Mead 1901–1978*. Washington, DC: National Academy of Sciences. Retrieved from http://www.nasonline.org/publications/biographical-memoirs/memoir-pdfs/mead-margaret.pdf

Science.jrank.org. (n.d.). *Life cycle—Adolescence—Anthropological critique*. Retrieved from http://science.jrank.org/pages/9979/Life-Cycle-Adolescence-Anthropological-Critique.html

Generalizations

B3

What generalizations can you make about the interaction between personal characteristics and external influences, such as people or opportunities, on one's future? Write down at least two.

Classifications

B2

How would you depict the key influences of her career on a charm bracelet? What objects would you use and why?

Details

B1

What details in Margaret Mead's biography suggest that she is an important 20th-century figure? What personal and external characteristics led to those successes?

F3

Reflecting

Margaret Mead's life was one of adventure and breaking new ground in a field called anthropology. Her new ideas were criticized or debated, as new ideas often are. What personal characteristics and prior experiences allowed Margaret Mead to withstand this criticism and continue with her work? How might you use lessons learned from her life to plot out your own career or to practice at times when others don't agree with your ideas? Create a plan, listing the lessons you learned and how you will use them.

F2

Monitoring and Assessing

Assess the role of education in Margaret Mead's life. What was the nature of its impact on her at different stages? How did her personal relationships and personal characteristics contribute to her professional life as well?

F1

Planning and Goal Setting

Based on Margaret Mead's life, what advice would you give to someone wanting to become an anthropologist today?

MARGARET MEAD

Lin-Manuel Miranda
Composer, Playwright, and Lyricist

Lin-Manuel Miranda is an actor, performer, composer, writer, and lyricist known for his work on the Broadway musicals *Hamilton* and *In the Heights*, as well as his work in television and movies, including the animated film *Moana*. His stage productions blend elements of contemporary music, like hip-hop and rap, with more traditional musical theater, while also allowing a space for minority actors and artists to shine. His productive and celebrated career serves as an example of what young people can accomplish when they value and cultivate their passions from an early age.

Lin-Manuel was born in 1980 in New York City, NY, to parents of Puerto Rican background. His father was a political consultant to New York mayors, and his mother was a clinical psychologist. He grew up in a largely Hispanic neighborhood in northern Manhattan. At home, his parents encouraged his interest in music; he and his sister took piano lessons, and the house was filled with the sounds of show tunes and salsa dancing. The variety of musical genres he heard at home influenced Lin-Manuel, who also enjoyed hip-hop, R&B, and rap music for their emphasis on rhythm and syncopation.

Lin-Manuel attended his first Broadway musical, *Les Misérables*, at 7 years old, which left a lasting impression and encouraged his love of theater. Although the family could not afford to see shows on a regular basis, they had a vast collection of Broadway musical recordings, and Lin-Manuel quickly grew to love musicals like *Cats*, *The Phantom of the Opera*, and *Jesus Christ Superstar*, among others. He had a talent for memorizing lyrics, which served him later, when he began acting in school stage productions as a preteen and teenager. In high school, Lin-Manuel played the lead roles in *The Pirates of Penzance* and *Godspell*, and became an important figure in the school drama program, even directing a production of *West Side Story*. He also met Stephen Sondheim during this time, a famous composer in musical theater known for his work on *Into the Woods* and *Sweeney Todd*. Sondheim was an inspiration and mentor for Lin-Manuel, and the two continued to correspond as Lin-Manuel's career developed.

After high school, Lin-Manuel attended Wesleyan University, where he studied acting and performed in many stage productions, including appearing as Jesus in *Jesus Christ Superstar*. He also began writing his first musical; he had been writing plays since high school, but they were mostly short compositions. He graduated in 2002, and spent some time teaching, acting, and performing with a hip-hop improvisation group.

In 2007, his first musical, *In the Heights*, debuted. A year later, its popular reception brought it to Broadway. Lin-Manuel wrote the music and lyrics, and starred in the show, which is set in Washington Heights, a largely Hispanic neighborhood in New York City quite similar to the one Lin-Manuel grew up in. The show featured hip-hop and Latin sounds combined with more typical musical show tunes. It ran for 2 years and received much acclaim, winning four Tony Awards, including one for best musical.

During this time, Lin-Manuel also worked on several lesser known projects. He did translation work for a 2009 production of *West Side Story*. He wrote the music and lyrics for 2012's *Bring It On: The Musical*. In addition to theater work, he appeared in television screen work, including shows like *How I Met Your Mother* and *Modern Family*, and in movies such as *The Odd Life of Timothy Green*.

After the success of *In the Heights*, Lin-Manuel became interested in the historical figure Alexander Hamilton. He read a biography of the American founding father and noticed some exciting themes from Hamilton's life that he wanted to explore. Hamilton was born on an obscure Caribbean island but grew to be a vital part of American history as the first Secretary of the Treasury. In Hamilton's experiences, Lin-Manuel saw a story of humble beginnings not so different from the stories of famous rappers like Jay-Z and Eminem.

He began working on a musical about Hamilton in 2008, presenting a song the next year and then continuing to write. In 2015, *Hamilton* debuted and was met with such immediate and widespread acclaim that it moved to Broadway just a few months later. The musical presents some of the historical events of Hamilton's life, including his relationships and his famous duel with Aaron Burr—the fight that ended his life. The musical is unique in its racially diverse cast, with many Black and Latino members, and its hip-hop and R&B sounds. These unique components challenged the common understanding of what musical theater can do, lending fresh energy to a historical topic and making the American Revolution relatable to today's audience. Lin-Manuel himself played the lead role, bringing a depth and excitement to the character. *Hamilton* quickly became a must-see event, with high-profile viewers like President Barack Obama.

Reprinted from public domain.
https://en.wikipedia.org/wiki/Lin-Manuel_Miranda#/media/File:Lin-Manuel_Miranda.jpg

In April 2016, *Hamilton* won the Pulitzer Prize for drama, and in May 2016, it received 16 Tony Award nominations, the most in Broadway history. It won 11 of those awards, including best musical and best direction, narrowly missing the record for the most awards (the musical *The Producers* received 12 Tonys). Lin-Manuel himself won two awards for original score and book.

Lin-Manuel also won two Grammy awards for *In the Heights* and *Hamilton*. After he appeared in his final *Hamilton* production in July 2016 (the show continued to run, but no longer with Lin-Manuel as the lead), he began composing music and lyrics inspired by the islands of the South Pacific. The lyrics and music he developed were featured in the film *Moana*, and the song "How Far I'll Go" was nominated for an Academy Award.

Lin-Manuel's influence has already shaken the theater world, as he helps to blur the line between Broadway music and hip-hop. Fans are excited for what he will contribute next, and young artists are paying attention to his work ethic and his ability to draw from diverse influences to challenge audiences' expectations.

References

Biography.com. (2017). *Lin-Manuel Miranda*. Retrieved from https://www.biography.com/people/lin-manuel-miranda-041416

Murray, L. (2017). Lin-Manuel Miranda. *Encyclopedia Britannica*. Retrieved from https://www.britannica.com/biography/Lin-Manuel-Miranda

Paulson, M. (2015). Lin-Manuel Miranda, creator and star of 'Hamilton,' grew up on hip-hop and show tunes. *The New York Times*. Retrieved from https://www.nytimes.com/2015/08/16/theater/lin-manuel-miranda-creator-and-star-of-hamilton-grew-up-on-hip-hop-and-show-tunes.html

B3

Generalizations

Write a generalization about the influence of a person's experience and interests on his or her future. Explain why your statement is valid using examples from Lin-Manuel Miranda's life and your own.

B2

Classifications

How does Lin-Manuel Miranda's musical style reflect his childhood experiences? Provide specific examples from his life and the music you selected.

B1

Details

Find and listen to at least three different songs from one of Lin-Manuel Miranda's works such as *Moana* or *Hamilton*. What patterns do you notice regarding his music and style? Compare your findings with others in your class.

LIN-MANUEL MIRANDA

Creative Synthesis

D3

Create a "recipe for success in a playwright career" by applying the information you have learned about Lin-Manuel Miranda and the other individual you researched in D2.

Summarizing

D2

Research another musical playwright of your choosing and compare that individual's childhood and successes to Lin-Manuel Miranda's. Summarize what you learned by making a list of influences, using the following headings as a guide: personal characteristics, barriers, access to opportunities of interest, failures, support from family or other individuals, and at least one other influence you found from D1.

Paraphrasing

D1

Highlight, in the text, the major influences of Lin-Manuel Miranda's life on his future success. Paraphrase each section you highlighted by writing a short statement or phrase in the margin of the highlighted text that tells about that influence.

LIN-MANUEL MIRANDA

Culminating Activities for Biographies

The following section has been created to provide additional challenge for gifted learners and their study of biography. These additional questions and activities are intended to provide connections across all of the biography studies read. These additional questions and activities may be used in discussion, as written work, or in centers during class time.

- Which of the six individual lives would you most like to emulate? Why?

- Examining only personality factors and the influence of significant people and events in the lives of these six individuals, who do you think was most successful and why?

- What internal and external motivators were present in the lives of all of these individuals? What do these patterns indicate about the lives of many successful individuals?

- How did gender, culture, income, ethnicity, and the context of the day in which the individuals lived influence their futures?

- How was the theme of overcoming adversity evidenced in the lives of each of these individuals? Why was this important to their success?

Select one of the following activities to complete.

- Write your autobiography as if you were at the end of your life, reflecting back. What significant events, experiences, and people heavily influenced your success from birth to where you are today? What challenges have you faced? What skills and personality traits do you need to develop next as you move to the next stage of life? How will you know if you are successful in your chosen career in 20 years? What criteria will you use to measure success?

- Interview someone who has been influential in your life or someone you determine to be successful. To what does that person attribute his or her successes? Be sure to ask about personality traits, significant positive and negative events, influential people, and life circumstances that have shaped this person. Compare this person's patterns of success with the six individuals you have been studying.

APPENDIX

A

Pre- and Postassessments

Appendix A contains the pre- and postassessment readings and answer forms, as well as a rubric for scoring the assessments. The preassessment should be administered before any work with *Jacob's Ladder* is conducted. Preassessments can be used along with the recording sheet to select specific ladders and differentiated instruction and also as a baseline for measuring student growth. After all readings and questions have been answered, the postassessment can be administered to track student improvement on the ladder skill sets.

Pretest

Emily Dickinson Poem

This is my letter to the world,
That never wrote to me,—
The simple news that Nature told,
With tender majesty.
Her message is committed
To hands I cannot see;
For love of her, sweet countrymen,
Judge tenderly of me!

Preassessment: Questions

Read and answer each question, using evidence from the reading to support your ideas.

1. What does the author think about the world? Provide evidence from the poem to defend your answer.

   _____

   _____

   _____

   _____

   _____

   _____

2. What did the author mean when she wrote, "The simple news that Nature told, / With tender majesty"? Provide evidence from the poem to defend your answer.

   _____

   _____

   _____

   _____

   _____

   _____

Preassessment: Questions, *continued.*

3. What do you think this poem is about? Give a reason why you think so.

_____

_____

_____

_____

_____

4. Create a title for this poem. Give a reason why your title is appropriate for this poem.

_____

_____

_____

_____

_____

Name: _____ Date: _____

Posttest

Emily Dickinson Poem

There is no Frigate like a Book
To take us Lands away,
Nor any Coursers like a Page
Of prancing Poetry.
This Traverse may the poorest take
Without oppress of Toll;
How frugal is the Chariot
That bears a Human soul!

Posttest: Questions

Read and answer each question, using evidence from the reading to support your ideas.

1. What does the author think about books? Provide evidence from the poem to defend your answer.

   _____

   _____

   _____

   _____

   _____

2. A frigate is a small warship. Why does the author compare a book to a frigate? Provide evidence from the poem to defend your answer.

   _____

   _____

   _____

   _____

   _____

Posttestt: Questions, *continued.*

3. What one word best describes what this poem is about? Give a reason why you think so.

_____

_____

_____

_____

_____

4. Create a title for this poem. Give a reason why your title is appropriate for this poem.

_____

_____

_____

_____

_____

_____

Assessment Scoring Rubric

Question	Points				
	0	1	2	3	4
1 **Implications and Consequences** **(Ladder A)**	Provides no response or response is inappropriate to the task demand	Limited, vague, inaccurate; rewords the prompt or copies from the text	Response is accurate and makes sense but does not adequately address all components of the question or provide rationale from the text	Response is accurate; answers all parts of the question; provides a rationale that justifies answer	Response is well written, specific, insightful; answers all parts of the questions, offers substantial support, and incorporates evidence from the text
2 **Inference** **(Ladder C)**	Provides no response or response is inappropriate to the task demand	Limited, vague, inaccurate; rewords the prompt or copies from the text	Accurate response but literal interpretation with no support from the text	Interpretive response with limited support from the text	Insightful, interpretive, well-written response with substantial support from the text
3 Theme/ **Generalization** **(Ladders B and C)**	Provides no response or response is inappropriate to the task demand	Limited, vague, inaccurate; rewords the prompt or copies from the text	Literal description of the story without explaining the theme; no reasons why	Valid, interpretive response with limited reasoning from the text	Insightful, interpretive response with substantial justification or reasoning from the text
4 **Creative** **Synthesis** **(Ladder D)**	Provides no response or response is inappropriate to the task demand	Limited, vague, inaccurate; rewords the prompt or copies from the text	Appropriate but literal title with no attempt to support	Interpretive title with limited reasoning or justification	Insightful title, interpretive, and extensive justification or reasoning

APPENDIX

B

Record-Keeping Forms/Documents

Appendix B contains three record-keeping forms and documents:

- *Brainstorming/Answer Sheet*: This should be given to students for completion after reading a selection so that they may jot down ideas about the selection and questions prior to the discussion. The purpose of this sheet is to capture students' thoughts and ideas generated by reading the text. This sheet should act as a guide when students participate in group or class discussion.

- *My Reflection on Today's Reading and Discussion*: This form may be completed by the student after a group or class discussion on the readings. The reflection page is designed as a metacognitive approach to help students reflect on their strengths and weaknesses and to promote process skills. After discussion, students use the reflection page to record new ideas that were generated by others' comments and ideas.

- *Classroom Diagnostic Forms*: These forms are for teachers and are designed to aid them in keeping track of the progress and skill mastery of their students. With these charts, teachers can look at student progress in relation to each ladder skill within a genre and select additional ladders and story selections based on student needs.

Name: _____ Date: _____

Brainstorming/Answer Sheet

Use this form to brainstorm thoughts and ideas about the readings and ladder questions before discussing with a partner.

Circle One: **A3 B3 C3 D3 E3 F3**

Circle One: **A2 B2 C2 D2 E2 F2**

Circle One: **A1 B1 C1 D1 E1 F1**

Selection Title: _____

Name: _____ Date: _____

My Reflection on Today's Reading and Discussion

Selection Title: _____

What I did well:

_____

_____

_____

_____

What I learned:

_____

_____

_____

_____

New ideas I have after discussion:

_____

_____

_____

_____

Next time I need to:

_____

_____

_____

_____

Classroom Diagnostic Form

Short Stories

Use this document to record student completion of ladder sets with the assessment of work.

0 = Needs Improvement   1 = Satisfactory   2 = Exceeds Expectations

Student Name	The Wolf and the Kid			The Last Lesson			The Mouse			The Monkey's Paw			The Diamond Necklace			The Celebrated Jumping Frog of Calaveras County			The Lottery Ticket		
	D	E	A	C	E	A	C	E	A	B	D	A	C	E	A	C	D	B	C	E	

Classroom Diagnostic Form

Poetry

Use this document to record student completion of ladder sets with the assessment of work.

0 = Needs Improvement   1 = Satisfactory   2 = Exceeds Expectations

Student Name	Weathers	Sonnet 73			The Clod and the Pebble		Hope Is the Thing With Feathers			The Wild Swans at Coole				Joy in the Woods			Not They Who Soar		
	D	A	C		B	C	D	E		B	C	D		A	B	C		B	C	D

Classroom Diagnostic Form

Biographies

Use this document to record student completion of ladder sets with the assessment of work.

0 = Needs Improvement   1 = Satisfactory   2 = Exceeds Expectations

Student Name	Erwin Schrödinger		Amartya Sen		Harriet Tubman		Marie Curie		Margaret Mead		Lin-Manuel Miranda	
	A	B	A	B	C	E	A	C	B	F	B	F

APPENDIX
C

Alignment to Standards

Appendix C provides teachers with a guide to the content and themes within the readings. For each selection, a chart delineates the national standards addressed by the readings.

Standards Alignment
Short Stories

Language Arts—Short Stories	The Wolf and The Kid	The Last Lesson	The Mouse	The Monkey's Paw	The Diamond Necklace	The Celebrated Jumping Frog of Calavera County	The Lottery Ticket
The student will use analysis of text, including the interaction of the text with the reader's feelings and attitudes, to create a response.	✗	✗	✗	✗	✗	✗	✗
The student will integrate various cues and strategies to comprehend what he or she reads.	✗	✗	✗	✗	✗	✗	✗
The student will use knowledge of the purposes, structures, and elements of writing to analyze and interpret various types of text.	✗	✗	✗	✗	✗	✗	✗
Students will use word-analysis skills, context clues, and other strategies to read fiction and nonfiction with fluency and accuracy.	✗	✗	✗	✗	✗	✗	✗

Standards Alignment

Poetry

Language Arts—Poetry	Weathers	Sonnet 73	The Clod and the Pebble	Hope is the Thing With Feathers	Joy in the Woods	The Wild Swans at Coole	Not They Who Soar
The student will use analysis of text, including the interaction of the text with the reader's feelings and attitudes, to create a response.	✗	✗	✗	✗	✗	✗	✗
The student will integrate various cues and strategies to comprehend what he or she reads.	✗	✗	✗	✗	✗	✗	✗
The student will use knowledge of the purposes, structures, and elements of writing to analyze and interpret various types of text.	✗	✗	✗	✗	✗	✗	✗
Students will use word-analysis skills, context clues, and other strategies to read fiction and nonfiction with fluency and accuracy.	✗	✗	✗	✗	✗	✗	✗

Standards Alignment

Biographies

Social Studies and Science Standards	Erwin Schrödinger	Amartya Sen	Harriet Tubman	Marie Curie	Margaret Mead	Lin-Manuel Miranda
Social Studies Standards						
Culture	✗	✗	✗			✗
People, Places, and Environments	✗	✗	✗	✗		✗
Individual Development and Identity	✗	✗	✗		✗	✗
Individuals, Groups, and Institutions	✗	✗	✗			✗
Science Standards						
Science in Personal and Social Perspectives	✗			✗	✗	
History and Nature of Science	✗			✗	✗	

About the Authors

Tamra Stambaugh, Ph.D., is an assistant research professor in special education and executive director of Programs for Talented Youth at Vanderbilt University. Stambaugh conducts research in gifted education with a focus on students living in rural settings, students of poverty, and curriculum and instructional interventions that promote gifted student learning. She is the coauthor/coeditor of several books including *Comprehensive Curriculum for Gifted Learners* (2007, with Joyce VanTassel-Baska); *Overlooked Gems: A National Perspective on Low-Income Promising Students* (2007, with Joyce VanTassel-Baska), *Leading Change in Gifted Education* (2009, with Bronwyn MacFarlane), the *Jacob's Ladder Reading Comprehension Program Series* (2008, 2009, 2010, 2011, 2012, 2016, with Joyce VanTassel-Baska), *Effective Curriculum for Underserved Students* (2012, with Kim Chandler), *Serving Gifted Students in Rural Settings* (TAGT Legacy Book Award Winner, with Susannah Wood), and the Advanced Curriculum From Vanderbilt University's Programs for Talented Youth series (2016, with Emily Mofield). Stambaugh has also written numerous articles and book chapters. She frequently provides keynotes, professional development workshops, and consultation to school districts nationally and internationally and shares her work at refereed research conferences.

Stambaugh is the recipient of several awards, including the Margaret The Lady Thatcher Medallion for scholarship, service, and character from the William & Mary School of Education; the Doctoral Student Award, Early Leader Award, and several curriculum awards from the National Association for Gifted Children; the Jo Patterson Service Award and

Curriculum Award from the Tennessee Association for Gifted Children; and the Higher Education Award from the Ohio Association for Gifted Children. Stambaugh has received or directed research and service grants totaling over $7.5 million. Prior to her appointment at Vanderbilt she was director of grants and special projects at William & Mary's Center for Gifted Education where she earned her Ph.D.

Joyce VanTassel-Baska, Ed.D., is the Jody and Layton Smith Professor Emerita of Education and former Executive Director of the Center for Gifted Education at William & Mary in Virginia, where she developed a graduate program and a research and development center in gifted education. She also initiated and directed the Center for Talent Development at Northwestern University. Prior to her work in higher education, Dr. VanTassel-Baska served as the state director of gifted programs for Illinois, as a regional director of a gifted service center in the Chicago area, as coordinator of gifted programs for the Toledo, OH, public school system, and as a teacher of gifted high school students in English and Latin. She is past president of The Association for the Gifted of the Council for Exceptional Children, the Northwestern University Chapter of Phi Delta Kappa, and the National Association for Gifted Children.

Dr. VanTassel-Baska has published widely, including 27 books and more than 500 refereed journal articles, book chapters, and scholarly reports. Recent books include: *Content-Based Curriculum for High-Ability Learners* (2017, with Catherine Little), *Patterns and Profiles of Promising Learners From Poverty* (2010), and *Social-Emotional Curriculum With Gifted and Talented Students* (2009, with Tracy Cross and Rick Olenchak). She also served as the editor of *Gifted and Talented International,* a publication of the World Council on Gifted and Talented, for 7 years from 1998–2005.

Common Core State Standards Alignment

The following standards from both national and state sources are provided to demonstrate the relationship to the specific ladders in the Jacob's Ladder Reading Comprehension Program. Teachers may wish to reference them in planning for the Jacob's Ladder activities and to learn how the program may help address standards in fiction, nonfiction, writing, and career readiness. The tables also allow teachers to see how they may use clusters of standards across the grades 7-10 continuum to meet the needs of their students.

Cluster	Common Core State Standards in ELA-Literacy
College and Career Readiness Anchor Standards for Reading	CCRA.R.1 Read closely to determine what the text says explicitly and to make logical inferences from it; cite specific textual evidence when writing or speaking to support conclusions drawn from the text. (Short Stories: Ladders A, B, C, E) (Poetry: Ladders A, B, C, D, E) (Biographies: Ladders A, B, D, E)
	CCRA.R.2 Determine central ideas or themes of a text and analyze their development; summarize the key supporting details and ideas. (Short Stories: Ladders A, B, C, D) (Poetry: Ladders A, B, C, D) (Biographies: Ladders A, B, D)

Cluster	Common Core State Standards in ELA-Literacy
College and Career Readiness Anchor Standards for Reading, *continued*	CCRA.R.3 Analyze how and why individuals, events, or ideas develop and interact over the course of a text. (Short Stories: Ladders A, B, C, E) (Poetry: Ladders A, C, D) (Biographies: Ladders A, B, D, E, F)
	CCRA.R.4 Interpret words and phrases as they are used in a text, including determining technical, connotative, and figurative meanings, and analyze how specific word choices shape meaning or tone. (Short Stories: Ladders A, C, D, F) (Poetry: Ladders A, B, C, D, F)
	CCRA.R.5 Analyze the structure of texts, including how specific sentences, paragraphs, and larger portions of the text (e.g., a section, chapter, scene, or stanza) relate to each other and the whole. (Poetry: Ladders A, C)
	CCRA.R.10 Read and comprehend complex literary and informational texts independently and proficiently. (Short Stories: Ladders A, B, C, D, E, F) (Poetry: Ladders A, B, C, D, E, F) (Biographies: Ladders A, B, D, E, F)
College and Career Readiness Anchor Standards for Writing	CCRA.W.2 Write informative/explanatory texts to examine and convey complex ideas and information clearly and accurately through the effective selection, organization, and analysis of content. (Short Stories: Ladder D) (Poetry: Ladder B) (Biographies: Ladders B, D)
	CCRA.W.3 Write narratives to develop real or imagined experiences or events using effective technique, well-chosen details and well-structured event sequences. (Short Stories: Ladders D, F) (Poetry: Ladder D) (Biographies: Ladder E)
	CCRA.W.9 Draw evidence from literary or informational texts to support analysis, reflection, and research. (Short Stories: Ladders D, F) (Poetry: Ladders B, D) (Biographies: Ladders B, D, E)
College and Career Readiness Anchor Standards for Speaking and Listening	CCRA.SL.1 Prepare for and participate effectively in a range of conversations and collaborations with diverse partners, building on others' ideas and expressing their own clearly and persuasively. (Short Stories: Ladders A, B, C, D, E, F) (Poetry: Ladders A, B, C, D, E, F) (Biographies: Ladders A, B, D, E, F)
	CCRA.SL.4 Present information, findings, and supporting evidence such that listeners can follow the line of reasoning and the organization, development, and style are appropriate to task, purpose, and audience. (Short Stories: Ladders A, B, C, D, E, F) (Poetry: Ladders A, B, C, D, E, F) (Biographies: Ladders A, B, D, E, F)

Cluster	Common Core State Standards in ELA-Literacy
College and Career Readiness Anchor Standards for Language	CCRA.L.1 Demonstrate command of the conventions of standard English grammar and usage when writing or speaking. (Short Stories: Ladders A, B, C, D, E, F) (Poetry: Ladders A, B, C, D, E, F) (Biographies: Ladders A, B, D, E, F)
	CCRA.L.3 Apply knowledge of language to understand how language functions in different contexts, to make effective choices for meaning or style, and to comprehend more fully when reading or listening. (Short Stories: Ladders A, B, C, D, E, F) (Poetry: Ladders A, B, C, D, E, F) (Biographies: Ladders A, B, D, E, F)
	CCRA.L.5 Demonstrate understanding of figurative language, word relationships, and nuances in word meanings. (Short Stories: Ladders A, C, D, F) (Poetry: Ladders B, C, D, F)
Reading: Literature, Grade 7	RL.7.1 Cite several pieces of textual evidence to support analysis of what the text says explicitly as well as inferences drawn from the text. (Short Stories: Ladders A, B, C, E) (Poetry: Ladders A, B, C, D, E)
	RL.7.2 Determine a theme or central idea of a text and analyze its development over the course of the text; provide an objective summary of the text. (Short Stories: Ladders A, B, C, D) (Poetry: Ladders A, B, C, D)
	RL.7.3 Analyze how particular elements of a story or drama interact (e.g., how setting shapes the characters or plot). (Short Stories: Ladders A, B, C, E) (Poetry: Ladders A, C, D)
	RL.7.4 Determine the meaning of words and phrases as they are used in a text, including figurative and connotative meanings; analyze the impact of rhymes and other repetitions of sounds (e.g., alliteration) on a specific verse or stanza of a poem or section of a story or drama. (Short Stories: Ladders A, C, D, F) (Poetry: Ladders A, B, C, D, F)
	RL.7.10 By the end of the year, read and comprehend literature, including stories, dramas, and poems, in the grades 6–8 text complexity band proficiently, with scaffolding as needed at the high end of the range. (Short Stories: Ladders A, B, C, D, E, F) (Poetry: Ladders A, B, C, D, E, F)

Cluster	Common Core State Standards in ELA-Literacy
Reading: Literature, Grade 8	RL.8.1 Cite the textual evidence that most strongly supports an analysis of what the text says explicitly as well as inferences drawn from the text. (Short Stories: Ladders A, B, C, E) (Poetry: Ladders A, B, C, D, E)
	RL.8.2 Determine a theme or central idea of a text and analyze its development over the course of the text, including its relationship to the characters, setting, and plot; provide an objective summary of the text. (Short Stories: Ladders A, B, C, D) (Poetry: Ladders A, B, C, D)
	RL.8.3 Analyze how particular lines of dialogue or incidents in a story or drama propel the action, reveal aspects of a character, or provoke a decision. (Short Stories: Ladders A, B, C, E) (Poetry: Ladders A, C)
	RL.8.4 Determine the meaning of words and phrases as they are used in a text, including figurative and con-notative meanings; analyze the impact of specific word choices on meaning and tone, including analogies or allusions to other texts. (Short Stories: Ladders A, C, D, F) (Poetry: Ladders A, B, C, D, F)
	RL.8.10 By the end of the year, read and comprehend literature, including stories, dramas, and poems, at the high end of grades 6–8 text complexity band indepen-dently and proficiently. (Short Stories: Ladders A, B, C, D, E, F) (Poetry: Ladders A, B, C, D, E, F)
Reading: Literature, Grades 9–10	RL.9-10.1 Cite strong and thorough textual evidence to support analysis of what the text says explicitly as well as inferences drawn from the text. (Short Stories: Ladders A, B, C, E) (Poetry: Ladders A, B, C, D, E)
	RL.9-10.2 Determine a theme or central idea of a text and analyze in detail its development over the course of the text, including how it emerges and is shaped and refined by specific details; provide an objective summary of the text. (Short Stories: Ladders B, C, D) (Poetry: Ladders A, B, C, D)
	RL.9-10.3 Analyze how complex characters (e.g., those with multiple or conflicting motivations) develop over the course of a text, interact with other characters, and advance the plot or develop the theme. (Short Stories: Ladders A, C, E) (Poetry: Ladders A, C)

Cluster	Common Core State Standards in ELA-Literacy
Reading: Literature, Grades 9–10, *continued*	RL.9-10.4 Determine the meaning of words and phrases as they are used in the text, including figurative and connotative meanings; analyze the cumulative impact of specific word choices on meaning and tone (e.g., how the language evokes a sense of time and place; how it sets a formal or informal tone). (Short Stories: Ladders A, C, D, F) (Poetry: Ladders A, B, C, D, F)
	RL.9-10.10 By the end of grade 9, read and comprehend literature, including stories, dramas, and poems, in the grades 9-10 text complexity band proficiently, with scaffolding as needed at the high end of the range. By the end of grade 10, read and comprehend literature, including stories, dramas, and poems, at the high end of the grades 9-10 text complexity band independently and proficiently. (Short Stories: Ladders A, B, C, D, E, F) (Poetry: Ladders A, B, C, D, E, F)
Reading: Informational Text: Grade 7	RI.7.1 Cite several pieces of textual evidence to support analysis of what the text says explicitly as well as inferences drawn from the text. (Biographies: Ladders A, B, D, E)
	RI.7.2 Determine two or more central ideas in a text and analyze their development over the course of the text; provide an objective summary of the text. (Biographies: Ladders A, B, D)
	RI.7.3 Analyze the interactions between individuals, events, and ideas in a text (e.g., how ideas influence individuals or events, or how individuals influence ideas or events). (Biographies: Ladders A, B, D, E, F)
	RI.7.10 By the end of the year, read and comprehend literary nonfiction in the grades 6–8 text complexity band proficiently, with scaffolding as needed at the high end of the range. (Biographies: Ladders A, B, D, E, F)
Reading: Informational Text: Grade 8	RI.8.1 Cite the textual evidence that most strongly supports an analysis of what the text says explicitly as well as inferences drawn from the text. (Biographies: Ladders A, B, D, E)
	RI.8.2 Determine a central idea of a text and analyze its development over the course of the text, including its relationship to supporting ideas; provide an objective summary of the text. (Biographies: Ladders A, B, D)
	RI.8.10 By the end of the year, read and comprehend literary nonfiction at the high end of the grades 6–8 text complexity band independently and proficiently. (Biographies: Ladders A, B, D, E, F)

Cluster	Common Core State Standards in ELA-Literacy
Reading: Informational Text: Grades 9–10	RI.9-10.1 Cite strong and thorough textual evidence to support analysis of what the text says explicitly as well as inferences drawn from the text. (Biographies: Ladders A, B, D, E)
	RI.9-10.2 Determine a central idea of a text and analyze its development over the course of the text, including how it emerges and is shaped and refined by specific details; provide an objective summary of the text. (Biographies: Ladders A, B, D)
	RI.9-10.3 Analyze how the author unfolds an analysis or series of ideas or events, including the order in which the points are made, how they are introduced. (Biographies: Ladders A, B)
	RI.9-10.10 By the end of grade 9, read and comprehend literacy nonfiction in the grades 9-10 text complexity band proficiently, with scaffolding as needed at the high end of the range. By the end of grade 10, read and comprehend literary nonfiction at the high end of the grades 9-10 text complexity band independently and proficiently. (Biographies: Ladders A, B, D, E, F)
Writing, Grade 7	W.7.2 Write informative/explanatory texts to examine a topic and convey ideas, concepts, and information through the selection, organization, and analysis of relevant content. (Short Stories: Ladder D) (Poetry: Ladder B) (Biographies: Ladders B, D)
	W.7.3 Write narratives to develop real or imagined experiences or events using effective technique, relevant descriptive details, and well-structured event sequences. (Short Stories: Ladders D, F) (Poetry: Ladder D) (Biographies: Ladder E)
	W.7.9 Draw evidence from literary or informational texts to support analysis, reflection, and research. (Short Stories: Ladders D, F) (Poetry: Ladders B, D) (Biographies: Ladders B, D, E)
Writing, Grade 8	W.8.2 Write informative/explanatory texts to examine a topic and convey ideas, concepts, and information through the selection, organization, and analysis of relevant content. (Short Stories: Ladder D) (Poetry: Ladder B) (Biographies: Ladders B, D)
	W.8.3 Write narratives to develop real or imagined experiences or events using effective technique, relevant descriptive details, and well-structured event sequences. (Short Stories: Ladders D, F) (Poetry: Ladder D) (Biographies: Ladder E)

Cluster	Common Core State Standards in ELA-Literacy
Writing, Grade 8, *continued*	W.8.9 Draw evidence from literary or informational texts to support analysis, reflection, and research. (Short Stories: Ladders D, F) (Poetry: Ladders B, D) (Biographies: Ladders B, D, E)
Writing, Grades 9–10	W.9-10.2 Write informative/explanatory texts to examine and convey complex ideas, concepts, and information clearly and accurately through the effective selection, organization, and analysis of content. (Short Stories: Ladder D) (Poetry: Ladder B) (Biographies: Ladders B, D)
	W.9-10.3 Write narratives to develop real or imagined experiences or events using effective technique, well-chosen details, and well-structured event sequences. (Short Stories: Ladders D, F) (Poetry: Ladder D) (Biographies: Ladder E)
	W.9-10.9 Draw evidence from literary or informational texts to support analysis, reflection, and research. (Short Stories: Ladders D, F) (Poetry: Ladders B, D) (Biographies: Ladders B, D, E)
Speaking and Listening, Grade 7	SL.7.1 Engage effectively in a range of collaborative discussions (one-on-one, in groups, and teacher-led) with diverse partners on grade 7 topics, texts, and issues, building on others' ideas and expressing their own clearly. (Short Stories: Ladders A, B, C, D, E, F) (Poetry: Ladders A, B, C, D, E, F) (Biographies: Ladders A, B, D, E, F)
	SL.7.4 Present claims and findings, emphasizing salient points in a focused, coherent manner with pertinent descriptions, facts, details, and examples; use appropriate eye contact, adequate volume, and clear pronunciation. (Short Stories: Ladders A, B, C, D, E, F) (Poetry: Ladders A, B, C, D, E, F) (Biographies: Ladders A, B, D, E, F)
Speaking and Listening, Grade 8	SL.8.1 Engage effectively in a range of collaborative discussions (one-on-one, in groups, and teacher-led) with diverse partners on grade 8 topics, texts, and issues, building on others' ideas and expressing their own clearly. (Short Stories: Ladders A, B, C, D, E, F) (Poetry: Ladders A, B, C, D, E, F) (Biographies: Ladders A, B, D, E, F)
	SL.8.4 Present claims and findings, emphasizing salient points in a focused, coherent manner with relevant evidence, sound valid reasoning, and well-chosen details; use appropriate eye contact, adequate volume, and clear pronunciation. (Short Stories: Ladders A, B, C, D, E, F) (Poetry: Ladders A, B, C, D, E, F) (Biographies: Ladders A, B, D, E, F)

Cluster	Common Core State Standards in ELA-Literacy
Speaking and Listening, Grades 9–10	SL.9-10.1 Initiate and participate effectively in a range of collaborative discussions (one-on-one, in groups, and teacher-led) with diverse partners on grades 9–10 topics, texts, and issues, building on others' ideas and expressing their own clearly and persuasively. (Short Stories: Ladders A, B, C, D, E, F) (Poetry: Ladders A, B, C, D, E, F) (Biographies: Ladders A, B, D, E, F)
	SL.9-10.4 Present information, findings, and supporting evidence clearly, concisely, and logically such that listeners can follow the line of reasoning and the organization, development, substance, and style are appropriate to purpose, audience, and task. (Short Stories: Ladders A, B, C, D, E, F) (Poetry: Ladders A, B, C, D, E, F) (Biographies: Ladders A, B, D, E, F)
Language, Grades 7	L.7.1 Demonstrate command of the conventions of standard English grammar and usage when writing or speaking. (Short Stories: Ladders A, B, C, D, E, F) (Poetry: Ladders A, B, C, D, E, F) (Biographies: Ladders A, B, D, E, F)
	L.7.3 Use knowledge of language and its conventions when writing, speaking, reading, or listening. (Short Stories: Ladders A, B, C, D, E, F) (Poetry: Ladders A, B, C, D, E, F) (Biographies: Ladders A, B, D, E, F)
	L.7.5 Demonstrate understanding of figurative language, word relationships, and nuances in word meanings. (Short Stories: Ladders A, C, D, F) (Poetry: Ladders B, C, D, F)
Language, Grade 8	L.8.1 Demonstrate command of the conventions of standard English grammar and usage when writing or speaking. (Short Stories: Ladders A, B, C, D, E, F) (Poetry: Ladders A, B, C, D, E, F) (Biographies: Ladders A, B, D, E, F)
	L.8.3 Use knowledge of language and its conventions when writing, speaking, reading, or listening. (Short Stories: Ladders A, B, C, D, E, F) (Poetry: Ladders A, B, C, D, E, F) (Biographies: Ladders A, B, D, E, F)
	L.8.5 Demonstrate understanding of figurative language, word relationships, and nuances in word meanings. (Short Stories: Ladders A, C, D, F) (Poetry: Ladders B, C, D, F)

Cluster	Common Core State Standards in ELA-Literacy
Language, Grades 9–10	L.9-10.1 Demonstrate command of the conventions of standard English grammar and usage when writing or speaking. (Short Stories: Ladders A, B, C, D, E, F) (Poetry: Ladders A, B, C, D, E, F) (Biographies: Ladders A, B, D, E, F)
	L.9-10.5 Demonstrate understanding of figurative language, word relationships, and nuances in word meanings. (Short Stories: Ladders A, C, D, F) (Poetry: Ladders B, C, D, F)
Literacy in History/ Social Studies, Grades 6–8	RH.6-8.1 Cite specific textual evidence to support analysis of primary and secondary sources. (Biographies: Ladders A, B, D, E)
	RH.6-8.2 Determine the central ideas or information of a primary or secondary source; provide an accurate summary of the source distinct from prior knowledge or opinions. (Biographies: Ladders A, B, D)
	RH.6-8.10 By the end of grade 8, read and comprehend history/social studies texts in the grades 6–8 text complexity band independently and proficiently. (Biographies: Ladders A, B, D, E, F)
Literacy in History/ Social Studies, Grades 9–10	RH.9-10.1 Cite specific textual evidence to support analysis of primary and secondary sources, attending to such features as the date and origin of the information. (Biographies: Ladders A, B, D, E)
	RH.9-10.2 Determine the central ideas or information of a primary or secondary source; provide an accurate summary of how key events or ideas develop over the course of the text. (Biographies: Ladders A, B, D)
	RH.9-10.3 Analyze in detail a series of events described in a text; determine whether earlier events caused later ones or simply preceded them. (Biographies: Ladders A, B, D)
	RH.9-10.10 By the end of grade 10, read and comprehend history/social studies texts in the grades 9–10 text complexity band independently and proficiently. (Biographies: Ladders A, B, D, E, F)